THE ARCHAEOLOGY OF LOSS

Sarah Tarlow is a British archaeologist and academic. As professor of historical archaeology at the University of Leicester, Tarlow is best known for her work on the archaeology of death and burial. In 2012, Tarlow was awarded the chair in archaeology at the University of Leicester.

SARAH TARLOW

THE ARCHAEOLOGY OF LOSS

Life, Love and the Art of Dying

PICADOR

First published 2023 by Picador
an imprint of Pan Macmillan
The Smithson, 6 Briset Street, London EC1M 5NR
EU representative: Macmillan Publishers Ireland Ltd, 1st Floor,
The Liffey Trust Centre, 117–126 Sheriff Street Upper,
Dublin 1, D01 YC43
Associated companies throughout the world
www.panmacmillan.com

ISBN 978-1-5290-9951-5

1 3 5 7 9 8 6 4 2

A CIP catalogue record for this book is available from the British Library.

Typeset by Palimpsest Book Production Limited, Falkirk, Stirlingshire
Printed and bound by CPI Group (UK) Ltd, Croydon, CR0 4YY

Visit **www.picador.com** to read more about all our books
and to buy them. You will also find features, author interviews and
news of any author events, and you can sign up for e-newsletters
so that you're always first to hear about our new releases.

For Rachel, Adam and Greg.

And in memory of Mark, of course.

'Everything is held together with stories. That is all that is holding us together, stories and compassion.'

Barry Lopez, nature and travel writer, Facebook post, 30 October 2011

CONTENTS

AUTHOR'S NOTE

When you find your husband lying dead, you think you will not forget a single detail of that moment, but already there are some things I am not sure about. As an archaeologist, I like to get my facts right, and I will try my best to do so, but five years have passed since that day in 2016 and I am excavating my own unreliable memory. I cannot go back and check. When Mark died, two days after our youngest child's eleventh birthday, the radio was off. I am pretty sure of that. Why did he choose to die without the World Service? It seems out of character. Could he have been listening to something else? Was his laptop on? I am not sure. I did not check then, and now it is too late.

1

THE SICKE MANNES SALVE

My whole adult life, I have made a study of death. Professionally, I am immersed in it. I have written about how people died in the past, and how the still-living thought about the death of their friends and prepared for their own ends. I am a professor of archaeology, specializing in mortuary and commemorative practices. I have written dozens of papers and several books about death, the dead, and how the relationship between the living and the dead changed between the late medieval period and the twentieth century. I teach classes on the archaeology and history of death; I have travelled the world giving lectures and research papers on excavated burials and standing memorials. I can tell you about the history of cemeteries or the growth of cremation; or talk about the places where people disposed of dead bodies by pickling them in alcohol, exposing them to the birds and weather, or placing them inside living trees. I can talk about the rituals of reburial and secondary burial. I have curated exhibitions and organized conferences on the topic, and written a PhD. On top of that, a few years ago, I trained to be a humanist funeral celebrant, so I developed a sideline in talking to newly bereaved people about the person they had lost, and finding the right words to say at non-religious funerals.

Even though I spend much of my waking life thinking about dead bodies and how people in the past have treated them, I do not find it depressing or ghoulish. I love archaeology. I enjoy the fieldwork, I like teaching at the university, I like finding out new stuff. Most of all, though, I love trying to work out what you can say on the basis of incomplete and inadequate data. As archaeologists, we only ever have a partial, unrepresentative body of evidence, without enough context – a few glimpsed and distorted details, never the whole picture, or even a sketch of the whole picture. That process of inference is what archaeology really is. People think archaeology is the same as excavation, but that is just a small part of it. Excavation is one way of retrieving evidence, but there are others; the art of archaeology is in taking all those bits of evidence – things recovered from below ground, standing remains of structures, traces in the landscape, microscopic traces in soil, bone or pot – and thinking about what they might mean, how we can use them to tell a possible – a plausible – story of the past. We never have enough evidence; we never know how representative our evidence is. To scientists in other disciplines, our data is rubbish. But it is all we have; we cannot generate more through experiments or trials. The fun lies in taking our terrible data and using it to say something interesting about people in the past. Our knowledge of the past is always incomplete, patched together out of material that is never enough, not quite the right thing and usually the wrong shape. My personal memories are not so different.

I am fascinated by the human understanding of death, the ways people make sense of it, and how the people left behind manage their relationship with the dead. I wrote my PhD about bereavement and the way that emotional relationships between the living and the dead, and the metaphors people use for death, have changed over the centuries. What does it mean, emotionally, to say that a person has gone on a journey, fallen asleep, gone to another world, is living in the ground, or has been reunited with relatives?

One question I have been working on since my PhD days is what archaeologists can say about the emotional relationship between the living and the dead. My partner, Mark, also an archaeologist, helped me find a way of talking about this epistemological problem, over many conversations that we had when walking in the hills, eating dinner or going about our lives. I remember one early exchange, while I was driving us home from Cardiff Airport after a long weekend in Paris. I had been researching the 'new', eighteenth- and nineteenth-century cemeteries of Montmartre, Montparnasse, Père Lachaise and Vaugirard. There was little to see above ground at the site of the old cemetery of Les Innocents, which had been cleared of burials in 1786, the exhumed bones taken by night, in a torchlit procession of wagons, to the disused quarries under the city. However, we were able to visit those catacombs, where the bones of the dead had been arranged into elaborate patterns and ornamented with wooden boards painted with quotations about death. Heroically, Mark forewent trips to galleries and museums in order to accompany me on my visits to the dead. On the way home, we talked about a paper I was writing on the archaeology of emotion.

'But you can't assume, can you, that people in the past had the same emotions that you do?' Mark said. 'That's just projecting.'

'I can't assume that people in the *present* have the same emotions that I do,' I answered. 'That's why this is hard. If all humans had the same emotional experiences and the same affective responses to things, there would be nothing to study. We'd already know. So the first hurdle is recognizing that people in the past might have felt differently – from me, and from each other. I can misread the emotions of friends and family, and they can misread mine. Come to that, I cannot even be sure about my own emotions half the time. Certainly not yours.'

'So, what hope could there possibly be of getting at the emotions of people from the past – especially the distant past, and when they haven't left us any written clues?'

'I think it must be to do with how a whole society values emotions, rather than an individual. I can't know whether you really love me, but I can see that we both live in a culture that values romantic love – look at all our films and books. Look at how we organize life around the romantic couple. We privilege romantic love at a societal level, and that's different from how other societies in different places and times have seen things. And when somebody dies, society has ideas of what the appropriate emotions are: grief, or anger, or fear. Whatever. So, even though I can't know exactly how a person felt, or feels, I think I can study "emotion" more broadly.'

'OK. You ought to know that I do really love you, though.'

The details vary according to anthropological or chronological context, but it seems that everybody wants a good death. Topping the late-medieval bestseller lists were how-to manuals written entirely with this end in mind – the *ars moriendi*, or art of dying handbook. These books are dominated by religious and spiritual concerns, and describe idealized, perfect deaths, with the dying man expressing theologically sanctioned hopes, fears and wishes in his last moments. The earliest *ars moriendi* books were published in the fourteenth and fifteenth centuries. They were immediately popular, not only with the monastic scholars who were the usual consumers of books at that time, but with the laity too. Latin originals were soon translated into German and French. William Caxton published an English translation, *The Arte and Crafte to Know Well to Dye*, in 1490. Books on the art of dying went on being published till about 1800. After the Protestant Reformation of the sixteenth century, both Catholic and Protestant traditions existed and continued to be reliable sellers. Indeed, the peak popularity of this kind of literature was not until the last quarter of the seventeenth century.

Thomas Becon was a sixteenth-century Protestant who held strong opinions on the theological controversies of his day and expressed them zealously. He fled abroad during the

Catholic reign of Queen Mary, but came back when Protestant Elizabeth I came to the throne. He wrote several religious books, but his biggest popular success was an enormously long *ars moriendi* text called *The Sicke Mannes Salve.* Sixteenth-century Britons could not get enough of it, and it ran to seventeen editions between 1560 and 1620. Apparently, *The Sicke Mannes Salve* had such a devoted fan base in its heyday that some people could recite the whole book from memory. It is basically a single deathbed scene, spread over 355 pages, recounting the last hours of Epaphroditus as he wrestles with the temptations that conventionally confront the dying man: pride, despair, impatience, loss of faith, and greed. Rather than the priests and liturgical rites of Catholic *ars moriendi* texts, the Protestant Epaphroditus relies entirely on the prayers and consolations of his lay friends to keep him on the theological rails. As he nears the end of his life, Epaphroditus experiences the disappearance, one by one, of his five senses; this is a part of the conventional narrative of death at the time. He asks his friends to prop him up a little in bed because, he says, 'I begin to wax very faint, and my breath decreaseth and waxeth shorter.' Soon after, he tells his friends that he can no longer see, and then that, 'As God hath taken away my sight so do my other senses decay.'

Next, he claims to have lost the power of speech, though that does not stop him from uttering pious hopes and prayers for several more pages. And finally, when he no longer speaks, his friend asks him to show some sign if he is still able to confirm his faith; Epaphroditus's last act is to lift a hand to show this, even when all his other abilities have left him.

People say that your sense of hearing is the last one to leave you. It is comforting to think that, even as the world slides from your grip like a wet bar of soap, you can still hear the normal sounds around you – a train going by, the washing machine working up to a juddering spin downstairs; maybe, if you are lucky, the voices of people you love. Maybe a radio.

Mark lost so much in the years, months and weeks leading to his death. Were his final minutes a shedding of the last senses and abilities that still remained available to him? One by one, system by system, the things that kept Mark anchored in the world had been taken from him. First it was his abilities – to drive, then to run, then to walk, dress and even go to the toilet. Next it was his very perception of the stuff of his life that was leaking away. Losing his sense of smell and taste not only derailed his professional plans, but also took much of the colour and joy from his life.

His ability to touch was not compromised – his fingers retained all their sensitivity till he died – but his capacity to feel gradually changed. Neurological tests charted his declining sensitivity to pinprick or vibration. At home, sensations that he had previously enjoyed or ignored – the touch of fine cotton bedclothes, for instance – became hard for him to feel, or he experienced them as pain or irritation. His skin felt constantly prickly or itchy. Because this feeling was produced in his brain rather than in his skin, creams and lotions did not eliminate the symptom, although the feeling of cool moisturizer being rubbed into his skin gave him some temporary comfort. At least twice a day, I rubbed body lotion into his back. I thought it was the lotion that mattered and the relief from itching, but now I think it was also the touch of human hands, and the alleviation, if only for a while, of being alone.

In the last few months of his life, Mark's eyes began to fail. Since his little stroke in January, he had occasionally had trouble with his vision. Sometimes it would seem to close in, as if he were about to faint; sometimes it would swim or dance. When that happened, he could not read, and even keeping his eyes open to look at another person could be like riding a fairground waltzer. With his eyes unruly, all he could do was lie in bed, listening to the radio, and increasingly that was how his light was spent.

Medieval and early modern *ars moriendi* books are religious books. They aim to prepare the Christian soul for death and give it the best chance of salvation. A good death in all these exemplary works is one where the dying person manages to keep to orthodox faith, carry out whatever prayers and liturgical acts are necessary and die calmly, without fear, and in steady hope of resurrection. The texts take us through the death of a man, sometimes called Moriens ('the dying one'). Most of the words are devoted to prayers and affirmations for the dying person, and catechismal questions and answers about death and resurrection. For a modern, secular death, there is little in all this religious stuff to offer our apprehensive mortal souls in our last days, but there are features of those *ars moriendi* books that could still model a good death for us.

The illustrated version of the most popular late medieval book has a woodcut showing a jam-packed deathbed scene.

At the centre is Moriens on his bed, but all round him are his friends and neighbours. As he dies, he opens his mouth and his soul comes out in the form of a naked child. Angels are on hand to receive his emerging soul, and, beyond our mortal vision, though perhaps not beyond Moriens's, a crowd of saints is observing this key moment. Whatever death was, for the medieval hero of the art of dying, it was not lonely. His friends, the consolers, have a key role in the deathbed scene, not only in keeping him on the theological straight and narrow, but also in comforting and reassuring him, warding off fear. They tell him how well he is doing, and that he is making a perfect end to his life. They keep talking to him, even after his ability to see and to speak has left him. They assume he can still hear. Moriens never has to die alone.

Medieval art-of-dying books are notable today for their lack of interest in explaining the death medically; they make no attempt to avoid or delay it. The Moriens character never dies *of* anything. His time is simply up, and he is about to die. That is all we need to know. None of his friends ever suggests that he should concentrate on getting better or that he still has many happy years ahead of him. This is, of course, a prerequisite for being able to talk about your own death with honesty and in detail.

Both Moriens and those around him know what to expect. Most of us no longer have this kind of familiarity with death, nor do we, for the most part, know how a normal death is likely to unfold. This state of affairs is completely different from the public and private discourse surrounding birth. I have given birth three times and each time I have had books to read and classes to attend, so that I could go into the experience knowing what would happen at different stages, knowing what might go wrong and how to put it right. I had checklists of equipment and supplies that would ease the process. I was advised to think about what music I would like to listen to, and to consider essential oils, or being in warm water, or getting a massage during labour. When the time came, I had my partner with me all the time, and a midwife who reassured me that I was doing well, that everything was going as planned. Yet too often we go into our deaths darkly and in fear. Even those who are knowledgeable and experienced in death often deny that it is coming. There is about death the whiff of failure and even of shame: a failure of medicine to restore health and youth; a failure of the dying person to fight hard enough or to have lived a healthy enough life; sometimes, a failure of those around them, for not noticing soon enough that an illness was taking hold, or for not getting the right kind of help. Guilt is endemic among the bereaved, who often feel that if they had only been more assertive with their relative or the doctors, if they had only tried a little more, loved a little harder, the death should have been preventable.

Many of my generation do not know what to expect when we die, or how we can control it. We fear that we will not cope with the pain, that we might conduct ourselves badly, swearing at the nurses or upsetting our families. We worry that death might happen to us when we are alone and helpless, or drug-addled and terrified. It is no wonder that Mark chose to keep control over the time and the manner of his death.

Perhaps we need a new *ars moriendi*, a handbook for a secular age. We need books not only to prepare for our own deaths, but also for some instruction and guidance on how we can help to ease the final days of those we love. Such a book would contain the factual knowledge of what happens in a body as it dies, and what signs we should expect to see. It would tell us what the experience might feel like to the person undergoing it. It would suggest things we can do or say to make it as good as it can be. I have not been present at either of the deaths closest to me. My brother and I, driving to Northallerton together, got to the hospital an hour after my father died, although my mother and sister had been with him throughout. In an expression of colossal bravery, to keep me safe from prosecution, Mark died alone. His choice, but not his preference.

In the medieval art-of-dying books, the dying person does not wait passively for things to happen to him. He is actively dying. He has the starring role. Having a good death is within his control. At the time those books were written, suicide was a civil as well as a religious crime. To end one's own life was to succumb to despair, to appropriate a decision that was rightly God's and to reject the natural and divinely ordered way of things. But our modern *ars moriendi* must make some provision for control over the process of our own ending. Because we have the medical knowledge that makes this possible, and because we no longer have an obligation to follow a medieval religious code, the kind of control we have will not be the same as Moriens's. When my time comes, I think I want somebody who loves me to sit by my side and remind me that I have mattered, that I will be, at least for a while, remembered, that the world is a different place because I have been in it. I want to hear the sounds of my house or of the season, birdsong or rain, wind or traffic. I want to know that my children will be OK, that my friends love me. I want to hope I can be forgiven for the wrong or hurtful things I have done, and for the things I failed to do that I ought to have done. I want more than anything to be forgiven for not making that kind of an end for Mark.

Mark sent his last text around midnight. He did not explain what he was doing: that would have meant I would either have had to call an ambulance and stop him, which I knew he did not want, or go to court for failing to prevent his death, or aiding and abetting suicide.

I know it will make me cry, but I cannot stop imagining his last hours. Did he feel calm as he arranged the notes on his table? Was he frightened? What were his last thoughts, his last memories? Why was the radio switched off? This was rare for Mark. For all the time I knew him, he was a radio obsessive, and found it hard to fall asleep without the World Service talking to him through the night. Years earlier, he bought a little speaker that went under his pillow so that he could listen to the radio all night without disturbing me – though, whenever I woke in the night, I could still hear its tinny, muffled voice or the faint ghost of 'Sailing By', the music that plays at quarter to one every night when Radio 4 offers up the last shipping forecast of the day and cedes its wavelength to the World Service. When he fell ill, that radio became everything to him: his connection to the world outside his bedroom, the foundation of all his conversation, his truest, most patient and tireless companion, when the rest of us, myself included, had fallen short. So why did he turn it off? Did he want to focus on his thoughts? Was he thinking ahead to my return, and planning that the silence from his bedroom would warn me what I might find in there? Was he just, committed environmentalist that he was, trying to save electricity?

So, he texted me, turned off the radio and then, I suppose, swallowed the pentobarbital with water. The effect of the drug is quick. He would have been asleep within a few minutes, dead probably within an hour.

Did he think of me? Did he feel alone, abandoned? Did he call for me, for his mother, for anyone to hold his hand while the darkness filtered in?

I cannot bear the thought, but nor can I drive it from my mind.

2

OTHER WAYS OF TELLING

At about 9.15 on the morning of 7 May 2016, I came home and found my husband of two weeks, my partner of eighteen years, dead in bed. It was a Saturday.

Still, I go over and over the way that morning unfolded. I woke at my brother Ben's house. Since I had left Mark alone overnight for the first time in months, and because he could not get his own breakfast or medication, I set off to drive home as soon as I was dressed and had drunk a cup of tea. Ben was going to bring the boys home in the evening. I texted Mark to say I was setting off, but I got no reply. Like the previous day, it was gloriously warm and sunny, and my drive along the empty A1 was easy and quick. I parked the car and walked up to the front door. There was a box outside – some stationery I had ordered – and, of course, Mark would not have been able to answer the door. I let myself in, put the box in the hall and shouted up, 'Hello. I'm home!'

No answer.

'Mark?' I started up the stairs. It was quite silent. I had a sick, empty feeling, as though all the organs in my abdomen had suddenly dropped about a foot. I sort-of knew, but I did not absolutely know. Not yet. I thought to myself, This is the last moment before our world changes; these are the last steps in my old life.

His bedroom door was open, as it usually was, so he could hear the sounds of the house, of the family. He found comfort even in the swill and roll of the dishwasher, the muffled chat of the radio in the kitchen. But, really, I knew before I went into the room; before I took that last step out of our life together and into widowhood, I knew what had happened. I remember most of all how he looked in the bed, lying on his back, wearing a grey T-shirt, the yellow duvet pulled up to his chest. His eyes were closed, his jaw slack, his skin the colour of a drizzly sky. He was absolutely still. Both wholly Mark and wholly dead. Oh, Mark. Oh, darling.

The police officer who arrived later that morning needed me to identify the body.

'Can you confirm that this man was Mark Pluciennik, your husband?'

I knew this body so well, and yet it was so altered from the Mark I had known at his most alive. This is not Mark, not really. It is just a kind of armature of him. As the illness progressed, layers of Mark as he was when he was whole came away: first the layers of paint and polish flaked off, and then the sharp corners were abraded; he became a little less defined. The joy and humour eroded away, his thoughtful intelligence contracted to a kind of brutal core. Next, his physical vitality, his confident strength seeped out of him, and then, finally, all that survived was this pared-down essence. Mark, without even his bruising self-assurance. Just pain, and love and courage.

And, now, not even that. Just memories. Stories. Stories and compassion.

At the start of our relationship, in the days of the Paris trip, I was finishing a book about the archaeology of emotion; Mark was working on a paper called 'Archaeological narratives and other ways of telling'. The way we interpret and present the past, he told me, depends on sewing together the scraps that we have into stories. Just like fiction writers, we use plots, characters and events to make a narrative. All the issues in archaeology that examine 'the origins of . . .' or 'the evolution of . . .' or 'the transformation from something to something else' are the playing-out of storylines with which we are already familiar. He himself was fascinated by the period at the interface between the Mesolithic and the Neolithic, when people adopted new technologies like making pottery, took up agriculture as the main basis of their economy, in place of hunting, gathering and fishing, and started living in more settled and larger communities. In Europe, there has been much discussion about how much of the social and cultural change was due to the spread of new populations and how much to changing ideas and beliefs. What kinds of interactions between groups of people and between people and their environment were most important in explaining the changes we can observe in people's way of life? Mark, however, wanted to know whether theories developed for understanding literature, folklore or history might also illuminate the way that archaeologists talk about the Mesolithic–Neolithic transition. Our characters,

he said, include things such as archaeological cultures, identified and usually named for their distinctive material
practices: Linear Pottery households, for example, or
Mesolithic hunter-gatherers. Our events and incidents are
agglomerations of little happenings that cohere into something which is bounded in time and space. An event might
be a war, or a large movement of people, or a sustained period
of colder-than-usual weather. Plots are complicated. Plots
are what turn a simple chronicle of sequential events into a
story. Plots impose order and coherence upon the jumble of
happenings that make a life, a century, an epoch. We could
always select different moments, different events, or organize
them in a different way. This does not mean that we make
things up or that we can say anything we like, but it does
mean that it is too simplistic to say that a narrative about
the past is ever definitively true. You could always tell another
story. Our archaeological narratives are post-hoc construc-
tions, built out of tiny elements like the presence or absence
of a single potsherd, the bone of a domesticated animal or
a solitary cereal grain.

You could tell a story about the origins of agriculture,
Mark explained, that would be a tragedy, a narrative about
how a more egalitarian golden age was ruined by a system
that let inequality thrive. The villains are self-aggrandizing
operators and wheeler-dealers, given the means, by the end
of the Neolithic, to promote themselves and keep the rest
of us down. Agriculture, in this story, is a technology that
released not only the potential for things to get better, but
also for things to get very much worse, like splitting the

atom. The spilt milk that will not go back into the glass. Or our narrative might be a romance, our protagonists the clever and determined individuals who eventually triumph by making possible a new, more expansive, more sophisticated way of life. It is hard for us to avoid telling stories that are already in some ways familiar. We recognize the tropes; we know what we want and expect to hear. And what story am I telling now, from this bit of far-more-recent past? The tropes of what is reductively called a grief memoir favour a tragic romance, a love story. But this is not a grief memoir. And, although there is love in this story, it is certainly not a romance.

Stories and compassion: here is a story that haunts me – Charles Dickens's *A Tale of Two Cities*. Lots of people know this one. It has a romantic hero and a selfless heroine, but those are not the most interesting characters for me.

Sydney Carton is a drinker and a cynic. His sharp wit and quick mind have brought him little personal success, though they have been exploited in furthering the careers of others. His abrasive manner and lack of social polish have left him, in middle life, a solitary and rather pitiable man. Into this disappointing life comes Lucie Manette, a beautiful (aren't they all?), gentle, kind young woman, devoted to her elderly father. Despite his cynicism, Carton is deeply affected by Lucie. He loves her with a passion that is almost, but not quite, enough to redeem and reform him. He knows he cannot be worthy of her love, however, cannot change his ways, and although he eventually declares his love to her, it is not to ask her to marry him, something he knows himself unfit for, but simply to offer his service:

> For you, and for any dear to you, I would do anything. If my career were of that better kind that there was any opportunity or capacity of sacrifice in it, I would embrace any sacrifice for you and for those dear to you. Try to hold me in your mind, at some quiet times, as ardent and sincere in this one thing. The time will come . . . think now and then that there is a man who would give his life, to keep a life you love beside you!

His love is selfless. He never hopes to have her for himself. He never changes his mind. He is constant. Lucie does not love Carton back, can never return his feelings. But she has compassion and kind feeling for him, because she is of that Victorian type of ideal womanhood which is universally kind and gentle. She can weep for him. Ultimately, though, Lucie's heart belongs to another man, Charles Darnay. Charles is all that Carton is not: charming, morally upright, pious. Less interesting, as is the way of the virtuous in stories, but Lucie loves him, and it is Charles she goes on to marry. The pain of rejection is compounded for Carton because Charles and he share an unusually close physical resemblance. Charles exemplifies for Carton what he himself might have been, had he not squandered his talents.

Years pass, and Carton remains a friend of Lucie and Charles. That is how he comes to be in Paris when Charles is caught up in the Terror of post-revolutionary France. As the son of a despised aristocrat, Charles is arrested as an enemy of the people. Lucie's father, a hero of the revolution, speaks in his favour, and for a while it looks like he might be spared the wrath of the mob, but he is rearrested and this time his enemies are implacable. It seems he cannot escape execution. At this moment, with Lucie close to despair, Carton finds the courage and sangfroid to fulfil the pledge he made to Lucie years before. He conceals his plan from his friends, lest they try to stop him, but instructs individuals in the parts they must play. He blackmails one of the guards to let him into Charles's prison cell, where he forces Charles to change clothes with him and uses ether to render him insensible. Then he has the unconscious Charles carried out of the prison, disguised as a drunk Carton. Charles is taken to where Lucie and her father are waiting in a carriage with another friend, who has been instructed to get them out of Paris and back to England as swiftly as he can.

When the hour of execution comes, none of the guards or officials notice that the prisoner is not the same man. Accordingly, Carton goes to the guillotine in place of Lucie's husband. It is an act of supreme courage and love.

I did not get round to reading Charles Dickens until embarrassingly late in life, although Mark loved his enormous novels. I used to be impatient with the phonetically rendered local accents, and the long and unnecessary subplots, but then, a couple of years before Mark fell ill, I heard a radio dramatization of *A Tale of Two Cities*. I downloaded the programme onto my MP3 player and listened to each instal-

ment on my long runs on Sunday mornings. I am a sucker
for Victorian sentimentality, and I eat up a grand, romantic
plot. Although I went on to read and enjoy other Dickens
novels, Carton remains for me the most compelling of all
characters, and his story the one that lodged in my mind in
the months after Mark's death.

Here is another story. This is one I tell over and over:

A man and a woman fell in love. She loved him for his
intelligence, his warm brown eyes, his stories. He loved her
for her quick mind, and how her face looked in profile. One
day, he reached into his chest, pulled out his heart and gave
it to her to keep. He never asked for it back. In return, and
because she loved him, she gave him her years and her loyalty.
Things were not always perfect. She could be sulky, resentful
and jealous. He could be arrogant, thoughtless and unkind.
But most of the time they loved each other. They cooked,
watched TV, raised children, grumbled about work, went
for walks, talked about the news, made plans and did the
crossword. Normal things.

One day, about fifteen years after they had met, the man
began to feel strange. Many doctors examined him, and saw
that parts of his brain were damaged. They did many tests,
but none of them knew quite what was causing this damage,
or what would stop it. More years passed. He felt stranger
and stranger, and worse and worse, and no cure could be
found. His illness made him itch and hurt. It made him cold
and miserable. It made his head ache, his feet clench and his
eyes fail. It took from him the ability to walk, or even to

control his bladder and bowels. It made him frightened and sad. The woman was worried about him, and about the future. Gradually, she came to do alone all the things they had done together: working, cooking, caring for the children, looking after the house. She was wrung out and often bad tempered. He was both grateful and envious. It made him cruel sometimes. Illness did not bring out the best in either of them.

The man saw how tired and anxious she had become. He saw how much the children's lives had changed. Neither of them knew how or when his illness was likely to end, but after a few years of deterioration it seemed inevitable that this story would not have a happy ending. He might die. Or he might live on – blind, immobile and in pain.

One day, the children wanted to visit their cousins. And, although she was worried and felt a bit guilty, the woman really did want some time away from the sickness and the scratchiness, to spend a soft summer evening drinking wine with her brother and sister-in-law, so she allowed herself to be persuaded. Accordingly, late one Friday afternoon, she set a tray with her husband's meal and the things he would need for an evening alone, took the children and left the house.

It was a warm, light evening in May, his favourite time of the year, and hers. The wife and children were a little giddy. They sang along with the car radio. Later, the children played in the evening sun, while their mother sat in her brother's garden and talked and laughed and drank wine. Later still, she went to sleep in her brother's spare bed, with his cats curled up on her feet. At about midnight, her phoned buzzed with an incoming text, but she was asleep and did not hear it.

Meanwhile, at their home, her husband drank his coffee and ate his food. He listened to the radio. Then he wrote two letters and left them on the table by his bed. Then, at midnight, he texted his wife to wish her goodnight, and to send love to the children. Then he took a fatal dose of pentobarbital, washed down with some squash from the flask, and, turning off the radio, he closed his eyes, lost consciousness, and died.

Some stories fall into our lives at just the right moment. Some lines from books stay in our minds because they answer, or maybe just articulate a question, a feeling, a need that was already there. In the months following Mark's death, I read the last chapter of *A Tale of Two Cities* again and again, until I knew it almost by heart.

'It is a far, far better thing that I do, than I have ever done; it is a far, far better rest that I go to than I have ever known.'

I do not believe people who say they have no regrets. They are either lying or they are psychopaths. My life is a series of regrets, and my conduct during the eighteen years of my relationship with Mark is the cause of many, but most of all I am so sad and sorry that I was not with him at the end, to hold his hand. In his book *Every Third Thought*, memoirist Robert McCrum wonders 'what is going to soothe those who are approaching their last exit? What story, or what words, will provide any real or serious consolation?' McCrum looks for the answer in poetry and essays, novels, interviews and memoirs. Death, whether contemplating our own mortality or turning over the experience of bereavement, often inspires great literature. When we try to find words, everyone's love sounds the same, but everyone's death is their own. Mark and I were both what he called 'wordy buggers', happiest expressing ourselves verbally, intellectualizing our feelings. But, at the end, there was no poetry or fine prose, no matter how euphonious, that would have eased his completion, unless they were words of reassurance and affection from the lips of somebody who loved him.

3

ARCHAEOLOGISTS WHO LOVE
TOO MUCH

The historian Jill Lepore once titled an article about the problems with the microhistorical approach in her discipline,
'Historians Who Love Too Much'. She argued that historians
who approach the past through the detailed study of single
individuals become too wrapped up in those lives and find
themselves allying with, even identifying with the subjects of
their biographies. As a result, it can be harder to reach a
balanced assessment of the past. Some archaeologists have
been excited by the possibilities of an analogous approach to
our own material, which may carry similar risks. The appeal
of microhistory is hard to resist. You start with a very close
examination of one incident, moment, thing or life, taking in
as much contextual detail as you can, and then spiral out from
that to examine wider issues of political, cultural and social
history. The historian Robert Darnton, a pioneer of this
approach, focused on an unusual incident when a group of
apprentices tried and executed their master's pet cats in Paris
in 1730. On that occasion, tensions had risen because the
printer's apprentices resented being treated worse than their
master's wife's cats. The cats, they complained, were given

better food and treated with more kindness than they were. The dispute escalated until the boys attacked the cossetted pets, held a mock trial and executed them. A small and strange incident, but one which Darnton argued was a symbolic act that played with a shared vocabulary of ritual and ceremony and expressed tensions not only arising from poor work conditions, but also a clash between the class culture of the bourgeoisie, in which animals were sometimes indulged with affection and comfort, and working-class culture, in which they were not. From one small incident, Darnton was able to move to big questions about labour relations, class identity, the function of ritual and ceremony, and the relationships between people and animals in early modern France.

I find this approach to the past appealing. It maybe has resonance for archaeologists because our material typically relates to small-scale incidents, or the lives and deaths of individuals. Or we might take a single artefact and try to write for it an object biography that could be a microcosm of technology, exchange, symbolic and practical meaning, change and obsolescence.

This is a seductive kind of theory for archaeologists. For a start, the unrepresentative and incomplete nature of our evidence does not matter so much. We can simply start with what we do have, rather than trying to make a statistical silk purse out of a sow's ear of terrible, unreliable data. By looking in forensic detail at a moment, an event, a thing or an individual and asking, 'Why did that happen? What does this mean?' we can start to link the local, specific and small scale to national or even global cultural patterns. My own story is really nothing more than a ragbag of moments, objects, pictures in my mind. One object-centre of my microhistory might be this electric hair-clipper. It is stored in a black zip-up case with a range of clip-on combs that hold the hair at various distances from the scalp. Mark bought it from Argos in Melton Mowbray around 2004, when the barber in town, who used to do walk-ins for five pounds, put his prices up. Mark considered, rightly, that a basic shearing with the clippers was not very technically demanding, and a small initial outlay would quickly be recouped. Haircuts were to be carried out by me. I found the clippers easy to use and, besides, I had cut hair before and had improved considerably since my student days, when I managed to give one friend a Mohican that ran diagonally across his head. However, by 2004, my time felt already overstuffed. I worked full-time in a demanding job. I had two children and another on the way. There was work stuff, house stuff and family stuff. It was not that any of the admin jobs were very demanding or difficult on their own, but the sheer number of them, the keeping track and remembering, was wearing me out. All the birthday presents to be bought, wrapped and sent; the kids' clothes to monitor and replace; the clubs and classes to book, pay for and get to; the holidays, visits and appointments to arrange and friendships to maintain. It felt like nearly all that stuff fell to me already, on top of housework and laundry, and, no matter how small an additional job might be, I did not really want anything extra to do. Plus, I was peeved that he had not consulted me. This probably demonstrates a lack of empathy on both our parts.

Using this clipper, I cut Mark's hair for the rest of his life. When we were younger, I liked to run my hand over his short crop to stroke his warm head. I enjoyed looking at his small ears and neat hairline, neither of which are attributes I possess. As our relationship deteriorated, however, I took less pleasure in what the zoologists call social grooming. I stopped seeking occasions for physical contact, and then began to avoid them. Intervals between haircuts lengthened.

The clippers no doubt carry physical traces of Mark. Although I have used them in recent years to cut the boys' hair, I imagine there must still be tiny pieces of his greying hair at the bottom of the black bag. The clippers tell the story of Mark's financial caution, but also bear witness to a problem of communication or empathy in our relationship. And they could chart my decline from passion to resentment, anchor a microhistory of a union unravelling. The clippers, and other artefacts I still have, scaffold my memory, but also leave space for me to fabricate, to be the archaeologist who loves too much, who makes a history as she would want it to be, rather than as it was.

And so I have to keep writing or I will not remember. I have to keep remembering, because who else will? Already there are things that have gone, or nearly gone. The children are forgetting, or letting the whole sludge of memory crystallize into a few polished gems, made bright by the constant buffing of repetition, or preserved in photographs, unreliable witnesses as they are, like insects in amber. The children were young when he was well, though, and the days of stick collecting and bedtime storytelling are leaching from their minds. The youngest one, Greg, was six or seven when his father had his first seizure and began, though we did not know it yet, the long process of dying. If the children forget, and without my parents, and now without Mark, there are great territories of my own history that I share with nobody. No one can support my story; no one can confirm or challenge my recollection. Nor will those fading moments be recalled to life by having someone to ask, 'Do you remember that time . . . ?'

. . . when Rachel was on your shoulders and she was sick down the back of your T-shirt?

. . . when we looked out of the kitchen window and we saw a fox and two cubs just a couple of metres away, on the patio?

. . . when we had a nest of rats in the compost bin?

. . . when you got the phone call to offer you the job in Leicester, after we had been living between two towns for a year and a half, with you doing that four-hour drive every weekend?

. . . when you made *Rouladen*? Where was that recipe from?

. . . when I had that terrible scan and the baby had died?

. . . when I got a bumblebee trapped inside my sandal and you had to take it off on the terrace of the restaurant with me shrieking and everyone watching the drama?

There are times now of which I am the only guardian. If I do not write down the things he said, the things we saw, the recipes he cooked, then, when death or dementia claims me, they are wholly gone too. Sometimes I feel that I should have written down everything, because so much is already lost. All the conversations, the meals, the trivial events that make an ordinary life. Occasionally, a piece of memory snags on a rough corner of my mind and I know there was something, but I cannot find the whole story. What was that business with the forms from the tax office? Where was that place with the lake full of water lilies? I know – and I am sure about this – that there were happy years when he was vigorous and sharp, when he made me laugh and made me think, but so many of those diamond-bright, hard-edged moments are becoming soupy with time, mushing into the general colour of my old life. How can I find Mark or our relationship, our years as a family, in just a mood or a feeling, like the hangover from a dream? I wish my memory was better, and then I worry that this might be the onset of dementia. Not a promising start for a memoir.

Since his death, I struggle to remember what he was like before. Our earlier life together, although there were years and years of it, is hazy and distant, with only occasional marker posts: I see his face like a photograph, caught in an instant when he turned and smiled at me down a corridor, before disappearing around the corner, out of sight. I remember him frowning in concentration when he argued a point in the seminar room, half-illuminated by the beam of the overhead projector. I remember the lurid orange paint in the bathroom at Cwrtnewydd that he had chosen because he mistakenly thought I liked it, and how we decided to use it anyway. Incongruously, although I cannot seem to order our years as a couple, I remember vividly his old, grey Volvo that we used to call the clown car because, every time you shut the door, some other part of it would drop off. It was a temperamental old wreck that needed careful handling – not that I am in any position to throw stones. I remember having contractions in a freezing hospital car park the night Adam was born, waiting next to that Volvo while Mark squirted the engine with WD40 so that it would start again in the morning. I remember one spring morning in Wales, when Rachel, my oldest child, must have been two, going for a walk near our house and coming into a wood which was radiantly, vibrantly blue with bluebells. I remember Rachel running into them in delight, and Mark and I, unusually for us, lost for words at the spectacle, just staring, open-mouthed. I know there was happiness and love and disappointment, there were sweaty nights and in-jokes, deep and difficult discussions and quotidian trivia and gossip.

We were together for eighteen years, married for two weeks. Four houses. Two jobs each. This is what we thought would happen next: a big, cheap, old house in Lincolnshire, with an outbuilding where Mark would make salami. I would be working from home for at least half the week. Mid-mornings, he would come across from the shed, where he would have been mincing and mixing the meat, and we would have coffee together. He would have been listening to the radio and we would talk about the news. He would grumble about politics. In the evenings, we would watch TV or go to concerts. Some days, we would go for a walk or a run together; to begin with, we would often take it in turns to go out because of the children. When the children grew up and left home, though, we would go out together. We would take holidays in term time, sit in a cafe in Vienna. We would eat well and get plenty of exercise. We would go to the children's graduations and visit them in their homes. At the correct time, many years from now, we would be healthy grandparents. But that is not the future we got.

4

THE ARCHAEOLOGY OF LOSS

I first went to Orkney in 1991, the year I started my PhD. I went to study long-term change in how people buried the dead, with a particular focus on metaphors of death and how they were represented in material form.

With all the self-assurance and ignorance of a new post-graduate, I thought that a reasonable time span to take on would be early prehistory to 1991. At that time, the hot thing in archaeological theory was the issue of power and inequality in the past, using broadly neo-Marxist ideas and insights from structurational sociology to see how power relations were negotiated and maintained. Accordingly, I set out to study all the prehistory and history of death and its metaphors in Orkney over the last 5,000 or 6,000 years, which I would then interpret to show how burial and commemoration had been an arena for making statements about status, power and legitimacy.

The best laid plans. In the end, my PhD turned out very differently. For a start, Orkney's prehistoric archaeology has had decades of interpretive research, by much better archaeologists than me. I was finding it hard to see how I could contribute. At the same time, I found myself drawn to the wonderful collections of post-Reformation memorials inside St Magnus Cathedral in Kirkwall, about which almost nothing was written, and to the entirely unremarked grave-yard monuments which did not fit into the power and status story I had wanted to tell. Spending my days wandering round Orcadian graveyards, recording the inscriptions and sketching the stones, what was striking about most of the monuments was not their ostentatious statements of power, but grief, affection and sometimes bewilderment: the prevailing emotions of bereavement.

Gradually, tentatively, I found myself trying to shape another kind of story. I abandoned fashionable prehistory altogether to focus on more recent historical periods, despite my supervisor's warnings that I would never get a job. And, instead of the material culture of power, I wondered whether I could find a way to address the material culture of emotion. My new approach was not universally admired. Enthusing to the other PhD students about how we should not neglect grief, fear and love in our archaeology soon earned me a reputation as the Barbara Cartland of the archaeology department – a position only exacerbated by being female in what was still a predominantly masculine academic world.

Emotion studies in other disciplines can be broadly arranged along a spectrum, with 'psychological' at one end and 'constructivist' at the other. At the 'psychological' end of the spectrum are those approaches which understand emotion as a bodily agitation. It is located in the brain and in the actions of hormones, and is thus broadly shared by all anatomically modern humans as a biological function.

Indeed, some people claim that emotions are far from exclusive to humans. Dogs, elephants, rats and even fish and bees have emotions of this kind. At the 'constructivist' pole, emotions are not considered to be universal among humans. Not only does the emotional content of a situation change according to cultural context – so that, for example, travelling away from home might be considered a joyful and exciting experience in some cultures, a frightening and lonely one in others – but the actual emotional experience is learned and social. Such approaches are often closely linked to linguistic studies which show that emotional terms are used in ways that are not translatable across and between cultures. Broadly, these two approaches align more closely with either a biological and universal view or a cultural and contextual one.

Public policy is more readily influenced by an approach that assumes universality of emotion. So too is popular culture. Emotionally universal pasts underpin the success of costume dramas, historical fiction and even television documentaries, which use emotions of love, grief, anger and fear as bridges between modern audiences and past people, and where the message of essential continuity is prioritized. People in the past were just like us, is the message, except that they wore long satin dresses or furry bikinis. Emotional pasts are powerfully attractive, but risk presenting modern and Euro-American sensibilities as universal, which, anthropology tells us, they are not.

The truth, as usual, is more complex than saying, 'Emotions are biological,' or, 'Emotions are cultural.'

Emotions are both. They are experienced in the body and relate to real neurological disturbances. Whether we find owls frightening or cute, whether we find cattle dung a source of revulsion or veneration are clearly culturally learned. But the way we experience and value emotion is also cultural. Emotion is what gives taste, shape and smell to human experience. It enriches and makes meaningful our daily lives and our most significant moments. The challenge for archaeologists like me is to explore the variability of emotion in the past. If we find an ancient shoe in an archaeological context, it might tell us about ideas of the body, habitual activities, aesthetic preferences, technology, gender, trade and all sorts of other information. The least interesting thing it tells us is that people in the past had feet. Similarly, the basic identification of fear or love in the past does not advance us much. But identifying a period, place and a group of people as living in a climate of fear, or an environment where an ideology of loving family bonds was channelled into building cohesive groups, or conformity to certain beliefs, is an important conclusion that enhances our knowledge of the past.

Vedbæk is a well-to-do, suburban neighbourhood, a few kilometres north of Copenhagen. It has a harbour, several hotels and some smart restaurants that have good reviews on Tripadvisor. It is well known to archaeologists because, 6,000 years ago, in the place where the elementary school now stands, there was a cemetery. It was excavated in the 1970s. Among the seventeen burials was a young woman, aged about eighteen, buried with a baby. Given the ages of the pair, it seems likely that they were a mother and child who died together during or just after childbirth. What makes this burial so exceptionally poignant and affecting, though, is that the dead infant had been tucked in next to its mother, and laid on the wing of a swan. We cannot know exactly what the feelings were of whoever arranged these two bodies for burial 6,000 years ago, but it has an emotional resonance today, though its exact meaning is uncertain. The swan's wing is soft and beautiful. Swans and water birds seem to have had a special significance for Mesolithic Scandinavians. They travel over land and water: wherever it was taking the baby, it feels like it would be a good place.

While it is easiest to 'see' ancient emotions in the traces of death, burial and bereavement, even commonplace and prosaic objects can be freighted with emotional meaning. My friend and colleague Lin Foxhall is interested in the ways that places – or, for her, things – acquire their emotional accretions. For Lin, 'objects can become charged with emotion in their own right, as well as being manifestations of emotionally significant relationships'. She considers the case of loom weights in the ancient Greek world. Used for keeping the warp threads taut and vertical while weaving, a common, clay loom weight is not the obvious place to look for evidence of feeling. However, Lin's study shows that loom weights were feminine artefacts that belonged to and travelled with women and were inherited down the female line. In a patrilocal society, where women were expected to leave their birth families to join with their husbands, the loom weight was a little piece of home, tying a woman emotionally to her birthplace, to her mother and to her childhood and education.

I must have seen Mark before 1995 because I found out much later that we had both been undergraduates at the same time at Sheffield University; we even had close friends in common. In those days, Mark had been a heavy-drinking, womanizing, political sophisticate, with a taste for difficult jazz and black coffee. I was a hippy type with a heap of nineteenth-century novels, an earnest enthusiasm for environmental causes, a terrible haircut and a bed-by-midnight policy. We were probably not even awake at the same time. But the first time I remember noticing him was seven years after we graduated, when he got into the train carriage I was in, on my way to Carmarthen in Wales, from where I was going to travel on to Lampeter for a job interview. I had recently finished a PhD and was applying for my first proper academic job, one which would let me both teach and carry on with my research. My journey to the interview involved a train from Cambridge to London, and then another one from London to Carmarthen, then a taxi for the last thirty miles to the small, remote college in West Wales. On the train, I was prepping for the interview, reading all the job materials, memorizing the information from the prospectus, rehearsing answers to every question I could anticipate and going over my presentation. A man got on at Swansea, wearing black jeans and a cream linen jacket. He was slim, good-looking, with olive skin and brown hair that was starting to go grey. He looked clever, worldly, attractive.

When I disembarked at Carmarthen, so did he. We both wandered over to the taxi rank. He smiled at me. 'Are you going to Lampeter? I noticed you were looking at their prospectus.' It turned out, we were both being interviewed for the same job – a permanent post, teaching and researching archaeological theory. He suggested we share a taxi. I do not remember what we talked about that day. The normal small talk of strangers thrown into the strange intimacy of the British academic meat market, I expect. I learned that he had recently returned from a post-doctoral position in Rome and was living in London with his girlfriend, pumping out CV-enhancing articles and trying, like me, to land the top prize of a proper, permanent academic post. He was older than me, and about a hundred times cooler and more relaxed, with his canvas satchel, his roll-ups and his easy, long-strided walk. Talking to him about his work, it took me about five minutes to realize that the other interviewees and I had no chance.

The interview took the form of a presentation in the afternoon, followed by a dinner with all the staff of the department that evening, an event that I privately thought of as the ordeal by vol-au-vent, and finally a panel interview the next morning. At the end of my interview, I was told I could expect to hear the result in the next couple of days. Maureen, the departmental secretary, phoned me at home in Cambridge the next day to confirm that a man called Mark, whose surname she could not pronounce (he said it *Ploochenick*, though the authentic Polish pronunciation was different again), had been offered the job and had accepted. So that was that. The best man had certainly won, I was quite sure. I thought it was the end of that story, but, as it turned out, it was just the start. I had been the second choice, apparently, and, four months later, another job came up in the same department. I sent in my application the day before I was due to leave the country for some temporary work in the US. A month later, in a used book store in Galveston, Texas, I got a phone call from the head of department at Lampeter, telling me that it would be in my interest to come back to the UK for an interview, so I did. I was luckier this time, and, in the summer of 1995, Mark and I became colleagues.

Mark was one of the cleverest men I have ever known. He and I were two of about half a dozen new academic staff appointed over a two-year period, all young, energetic, full of ideas. All desperately showing off and trying too hard to prove our brilliance to one another and to our older colleagues. We were bower birds, setting out our shiny gewgaws of knowledge, our colourful arguments in a blousy display. Look at me! Admire me! Mark had a tendency to mumble, which irritated me at first, leaning his elbow on the table and propping his chin so that he spoke indistinctly into the palm of his hand, but his comments were sincere, genuinely informed and at the same time brilliant, making connections, cutting to the heart of what matters. We were young, ambitious, experimental. We were absurd and we were glorious then, charged with the zeal and confidence of our own inexperience. We set up new discussion groups, experimented with new ways of publishing, collaborated with artists and performers. We talked passionately about ideas, bent our necks over impenetrable French philosophers. We sat in one another's living rooms in the thick darkness of West Wales, or in the pub or the cafe opposite the department – what was its name? What comes to mind now is the Sausage Garden, but that cannot be right. On Sundays, we walked in the hills and, from time to time, shared the forty-five-minute drive into Carmarthen or Aberystwyth to see a film or a play. Once, we all went deep into the forest on a dark October evening to see a piece of experimental theatre, co-produced by our department's performance artist in residence – for this was the kind of department that had a performance artist in residence – in which members of a Welsh-speaking company swung from trees and scaffolding. It was heady stuff.

Thursday night was research-seminar night. There would be a guest lecture at five o'clock, a round of discussion, then everyone went to the pub for a dinner of chips, beer and more talking. One Thursday evening, about a year after I had started at Lampeter, there were about a dozen of us squeezed around a pair of small tables pushed together, which were crowded with half-drunk glasses of beer and unzipped packets of crisps. I sat nearest the door. Mark was at the far side of the group, perched on a stool, rolling a cigarette. In those days, about half the department smoked roll-ups. I was never a smoker, and was too much of a good girl to pick up the habit. In the pub that evening, he was wearing his usual black jeans and a grey jumper, sitting with his legs crossed. As he held the lighter to his cigarette, his face half-illuminated by the flame, the warm light touched his jaw and reflected in his brown eyes as he looked up at something someone had said. With a lurch in my chest, I felt a powerful desire to stroke his cheek. In a single, tumbling moment, I knew I was sunk.

At work, Mark and I were allies and conspirators. He had the habit – which was both flattering and unnerving – of listening very closely to what was said, especially if it had any theoretical, critical or philosophical pretensions, and, after a moment's silent consideration, coming back with a question or observation that showed he had seen to the heart of the argument, probed its weaknesses, evaluated its ingenuity, and now he wanted to draw it out. He was not interested particularly in the grand rhetoric of the lecture theatre, or in oratorical showboating, but he excelled in small group discussions. I suppose this is what made him such a good teacher, especially of clever postgraduates. Conversation with Mark was not relaxing, but I craved it. It felt like playing chess. I knew that he thought well of me. Occasionally he would make some approving remark to me about a piece of work I had done or a comment I made. I was desperately anxious that he should not find out how numerous and extensive were my areas of ignorance, or how slowly the wheels in my brain seemed to turn in comparison to his.

Mark's academic passion was for the transition from the Mesolithic to the Neolithic in Europe – the adoption of agriculture, more settled groups and the emergence of new technologies and significant modifications to the natural landscape, such as clearing land for farming and building megalithic monuments. When I asked him what the attraction of the Mesolithic was for him, he responded immediately: 'Forests. I love the idea that Europe was covered in trees. Can you imagine how those parched, bare, scrubby Mediterranean landscapes looked when they were blanketed with forest, with streams running through, and all the bird-song and the animals?'

His approach to archaeology was both supremely rational and indulgently romantic. On reflection, that was pretty much his approach to everything.

Mark loved thinking and writing, which is what propelled him towards academia, after an earlier career as a journalist. But he was also skilled at university politics. I would watch him in committee meetings, where he always seemed to see a clear way through the brambly undergrowth of academic regulation and cut to what was important. I admired him. I wanted to be like him. I wanted to handle myself with his conviction and quiet confidence. Unlike him, I was fearful of upsetting people, of looking stupid, of betraying my igno-rance or failure of understanding. I was young, female and inexperienced; he had the confidence that comes with expe-rience and with possessing those attributes of sex, race, age and education that give you natural authority.

If this gives the impression that it was only Mark's mind I noticed, that would not be accurate. He was handsome. Our friend Alex had a game to keep us entertained over coffee: which actor would play each of us in the film of our university life? Alex was Mark Williams, who plays Mr Weasley in the Harry Potter films; other colleagues would be Sigourney Weaver and Michael Douglas, and Mark, we decided by universal consensus, should be played by a young Robert Lindsay. He had the same brown colouring, with tanned skin, brown hair and dark, thickly lashed eyes. He had dense, interrogative eyebrows, a large but straight nose and chin. He had the kind of defined face that would grow craggy with age, rather than jowly. His body was athletic and muscular. He looked like a sportsman, although he never went to the gym – and I am not sure whether there was a gym in Lampeter at the time – and he did not run; he cycled only occasionally and took the odd weekend walk. However, like the rest of us, Mark spent the summer months every year doing strenuous archaeological fieldwork. His projects at the time were in Sicily and Albania. The time spent wielding a mattock, digging and pushing wheelbarrows under the Mediterranean sun must have been enough to keep his mesomorphic figure strong. He dressed casually, invariably in black jeans. In the summer, he used to wear a plain T-shirt and a cream linen jacket. In winter, one of about three jumpers he owned. One was knitted by a previous girlfriend, I later found out, and one had been found washed up on a beach in the Hebrides. Mark rarely bought any clothes and, having found a uniform that worked for him, he stuck with it for the rest of his life, supplemented by whatever he received as birthday or Christmas gifts. In 2002, when he got his job at Leicester, he resolved to try a new approach and bought two suits in the January sales. These remained largely untouched in his wardrobe. I gave them to the Age UK charity shop after he died, and I imagine they went into the nearly new section.

With our friend and colleague Yannis, Mark and I organized a conference in the summer of 1998. The theme was archaeological approaches to understanding human bodies. We called it 'Thinking through the Body'. We thought it would be fun to have an exhibition by local artists on the same theme running in parallel with the conference. Luci, a PhD student at the university who had lived locally for years and had all sorts of contacts in the villages round about, put us in touch with several local artists. A couple of students submitted pieces. The husband of a colleague in the modern languages department was a photographer and wanted to show some of his studies of the human body. They were currently in an exhibition in Swansea, however, so a couple of us would need to drive down and collect the photos, mounted on three-sided lightweight columns, each as tall as a person, and bring them to the university building where the exhibition would be held. The complication was that a number of the photographs featured a penis in various states of engorgement. Legally, we would need to ensure that visitors to the exhibition were warned about what was going to be thrust in their faces. We could manage the exhibition by putting the photographs in a separate room with a notice on the door, but the process of moving the display blocks would have to be carried out without risking shock and surprise to the innocent residents of Swansea, or anyone who pulled up next to the car on the A48. It was a long drive from Lampeter to Swansea and back. Really, I suppose it would have been possible for one person to collect the columns on their own, but Mark and I agreed to go together, so I could 'help'. I think both of us were glad to have a reason to spend time together. And the hilarity of carrying enormous pictures of genitals down the steep side streets of Swansea, trying to keep the concealing blankets in place, made it a fun afternoon. The ridiculousness of our situation only enhanced the flirtatious atmosphere. But, at that time, both of us were in relationships with other people, so, although there was some enjoyable, surreptitious eying-up, nothing happened. Not yet.

Our flirtation was intellectual and exhausting. In numerous and long discussions about politics, theory or philosophy, both of us were trying to show off how quick, how clever, how witty we could be. We must have been insufferable to everyone else. While Mark was a natural intellectual, for me it was hard work. Each conversation successfully completed without having, to my mind, embarrassed myself, felt like an achievement. I loved being in his company. He kept me sharp and made me push myself intellectually harder than I have ever done, before or since. I look back at the work I produced over that time, and it is the best of my career. But, when our conversations ended and we went our separate ways, the relief was like taking off a pair of heels that hurt my feet and stopped me walking normally.

The rewards of doing well at the game, however, were addictive. Mark's approval was not easily earned. He could be dismissive of arguments he found weak. But the occasional compliments he dropped on me, always about the quality of my mind, never my clothes, character, taste or anything else, were as sweet and moreish as caramelized nuts. I bathed in the delight of being bracketed with him when he talked about 'people like us', meaning thinkers and writers. I so wanted to be a person like him.

It was not until a few months later that things took a more decisive turn. Two of our friends had rented a quirky little house made of cedar shingles, quite out of keeping with the dominant vernacular of the town, which featured brick or breeze-block boxes with cracked and stained pebbledash exteriors, streaked brown or green from overflowing gutters and rusting pipework. Our friends' house, The Cedrine, looked out of place, like it had been deposited on its way to Oz, crushing the grim witch of Lampeter architectural style beneath it.

Their house-warming party took place on a warm evening, just as summer was turning into autumn. I was already there when Mark arrived. I felt nervous, on edge, and was drinking red wine to steady myself. I noticed the moment he walked in, of course, but pretended to be engrossed in conversation. He was good at this, too, and joined another group of people across the room. We barely spoke to each other all evening, though he was steadily chugging through a few cans of beer. I had left my car at work. My home was a couple of miles away, out of town on the Aberaeron road. A back lane would bring me from The Cedrine, past the old Falcondale hotel and through a forestry plantation, up to the main road, from where it was only about half a mile's careful walk along the verge to get back to my isolated roadside house. Around midnight, I got up to leave, both relieved and disappointed that I had barely spoken to Mark. The night was clear, and the moon a little past full. There was enough light, even on this unlit rural road, to find my way home. It was warm and pleasant, unusually still for normally windy Wales.

I had just said my goodbyes at the front door, when Mark came up behind our host.

'Actually, I'd better make a move too.' And, to me, 'I'll walk you back to the college.'

At the road, I turned left, towards my house, rather than right, towards town and the college.

'I'm not going back to the college. I'm going to walk home.'

'Well, I'll go with you as far as the main road.'

'You're not going to drive home?'

'Too much beer. I'll go back to the college car park afterwards and sleep in the car.'

Our arms brushed together as we walked along in silence, under a gibbous moon. Then his hand took mine. Neither of us said anything, but I smiled.

There were no cars. It was not that kind of road. We were well away from the few bungalows and past the Falcondale, coming into a patch of woodland, through which the lane wound upwards to the main road.

'For the last few weeks . . .' Mark began and tailed off. 'I mean . . .'

He took a deep breath and started again: 'I think this is it for me. The big one. I think about you all the time. I can't sleep.'

He stopped and turned to face me.

'If you kiss me now, I think I will just faint into a ditch.'

This was the glorious, wonderful, exciting, terrifying thing. At the top of the lane, before he turned to go back to his car, I tested it out. He did not faint. Thinking about it, I am not even sure that there was a ditch just there. I got back to my house too excited to sleep. I sat up all night, drinking tea and writing terrible poetry.

Mark was rarely, even in those early, dizzy days of falling in love, easy company. John Bayley says that, while his wife, Iris Murdoch, was a good person, 'I'm not good inside, but I can get by on being nice.' Mark was the opposite: a fundamentally good man with a keen sense of justice, but not always a nice one. He struggled with chit-chat and with the tiny, daily compromises by which we agree not to pursue difference of opinion. He could be abrasive and arrogant, and on more than one occasion alienated my friends with his argumentative and oppositional style. But he was also one of the least egotistical or vain men I have ever met. He was often angry with situations, especially politics, but never about personal slights, which he rarely noticed. He was unfailingly kind and patient with the people he managed at work, as with small children and the very old. He was polite to anyone with less power than him, including salespeople, cold callers or service staff, whom he regarded as the vulnerable and exploited victims of the capitalist system. He was completely candid, and though he was a private man and often chose not to share information, he never lied. His honesty was absolute and sufficient. That was why, I think, after he had told me that he was in love with me, he never felt the need to repeat it again. He had spoken. He told me, in fact, that I was the love of his life, and then he never said he loved me again, but it remained a true fact for him, even when my affections were faltering at the end, even when I was being grumpy and harsh and it was hard to see how anyone could love me. When he died, I found out his will recorded that, after a few bequests to charities and relatives, the remainder of his estate should go to Sarah, 'the love of my life'. I am sad he did not say that to me while he was still alive.

5

BACKFILLING

There is always health and safety stuff on excavation sites, rather more now than thirty years ago, when some pretty startling things used to happen, and it is a wonder that, in the main, field archaeologists who were active through the eighties and nineties still have the usual number of limbs. You could put a mattock through your foot or thwack a colleague with a ranging pole in a slapstick, workplace-specific variation on the clowns-with-a-ladder routine. But the greatest risk is that you, or another digger, or a passer-by, or an animal might fall into an open trench, and/or that the trench might collapse on someone. I remember working on a site in Ely in the early 1990s, where the first job every morning was to go round the open trenches and rescue any hedgehogs that had fallen in overnight. To prevent unnecessary hedgehog distress, and any more serious problems, as soon as a trench has been fully excavated and recorded, we backfill. Backfilling is the process of making the site look like it did before work started, the holes filled in and tamped down, the turf reinstated, the ground free of humps or hollows. The thing is, whenever I go back to a place where I know there has been an excavation, unless the site has been entirely obliterated by a new multistorey car park or a ring road, it is always possible to see where the disruption was. Backfilling never completely restores the site to what it was before. I have had only partial success backfilling my own life before Mark got ill. I am not wholly confident I can remember what the unmutilated landscape looked like any more.

I do remember one morning when Greg, the youngest one, was about three or four, I was driving to work past the Methodist church just as the mothers and toddlers were arriving for playgroup. I thought about what it would be like to sit in a plastic chair in the church hall, drinking tea and chatting. Then to wander home and get soup and bread for our lunch, before, perhaps, a trip to the park to feed the ducks. It sounded brilliant. By that time, we had moved to new jobs at Leicester University: mine as a teaching and research academic; Mark managing the archaeology distance-learning programme and maintaining a research career at the same time. We lived in a comfortable house in Melton Mowbray, both worked full-time and filled up every other crevice of our lives with looking after the three children and keeping up with the shopping, housework and the unremark-able business of living.

I loved my job and I still do. I knew I was fortunate to be able to make a living from doing what I enjoyed, but work was smothering the rest of our lives. Wouldn't it be nice, I thought, to have the space in my days to spend relaxed time with the kids, to feel on top of the chores, maybe even to do some of the other things I enjoy? Could I maybe do the same work, but just a bit less of it? For the next few days, I could not shake that tantalizing glimpse of another way of parenting, a different lifestyle. Since my first job in Lampeter, I had worked full-time, and in quite a difficult professional role that often spilled over into weekends and evenings. I had taken only my paid periods of maternity leave and had gone back to work just a few months after each child was born. I do not feel guilty that my children went to nursery, and I hate the way that women with children feel forced to defend their choices all the time. Full-time, stay-at-home motherhood was not for me, but full-time, rarely-at-home professionalism was not ideal either. What kept me working full-time was that I knew of only one person at work who had moved to a part-time contract, and her career had stalled as a result. My suspicion was that, in the world of academia at the time, where part-time work was hardly known and our contracts did not even specify working hours, I would end up working nearly full-time anyway, and just be paid less. What is half of an amorphous and unbounded blot of a job?

I also worried about what it would mean for our relationship if I were to give my career less importance. Mark loved being the partner of a successful career woman. He could sometimes be dismissive about women who had 'given up'. I had invested quite a bit of effort in being the kind of woman Mark would admire, and while that was not the only factor driving my work life, it was significant. Would our partnership survive us adopting more traditional gender roles?

That morning, though, a life spacious enough to take my little boy to playgroup on a weekday morning seemed both desperately desirable and an entirely reasonable expectation. How had I ended up with the kind of job and the kind of life where that work pattern had come to seem impossible? I brooded and fermented. Would I be able to organize something like that?

I asked Mark what he thought about the possibility of me reducing my working hours, to give me more time with the kids and also, I hoped, to feel less frazzled. He responded as I suspected he would: it would not work. Being an academic is something you are, not something you do; it is not a quantifiable job. What is 0.6 of that? I would be offering myself up for exploitation. But, a couple of days later, he came back to me with another suggestion. How about, he asked, we both work like mad for a couple of years, live frugally and squirrel away as much money as possible, then jump out of academic life altogether and live differently? If I could hold out just a little longer, something much better might be possible. It was an exciting idea. Working at a British university had become stressful and demanding. I still loved teaching students and doing my own research, but I had less and less freedom in how I went about my core activities, and was increasingly subject to a tyranny of best practice. How appealing, then, was the vision of a working life in which Mark and I could make our own decisions, set our own priorities. Part of me still wanted to make a change sooner than that, and, deep down, I thought that the extra vigilance required to keep my working hours down might be a price worth paying in order to reclaim some of my time from the university, but I did not want to risk losing Mark's esteem by becoming the kind of plodding mum with a wife's job I knew would disappoint him.

Our plans started to take shape. In 2011, Leicester University announced a call for voluntary redundancies and early retirements. It seemed the right moment for Mark to jump ship, so he applied for the scheme and, later that year, left the university. We had, for the last couple of years, been spending our evenings researching possible places to live, looking for that enchanted intersection of decent schools, cheap property and reasonable proximity to markets for whatever income-generating activity we decided on. Mark pointed out that, if we moved to Lincolnshire, we ought to be able to find somewhere that met all those criteria. We drew up a shortlist of Lincolnshire towns. Were there things for the kids to do? Would we be able to make friends here? Was there pretty countryside nearby? Could we live here? Those few months, after we had decided to leave the university, and while we were making our plans and going on our voyages of discovery, stand in my mind now as one of the happiest times in our relationship. We would take a day's holiday from work, drop the children at school and then drive off to a new place that neither of us knew, spend the day shopping for a fantasy future, having time together without children, work or other pressures. As it turned out, that was the last sustained period of optimism for us, but at the time it felt like a new beginning, not an ending. The work pressure that made Mark sometimes short-tempered and miserable had gone, we were both fit and running regularly, the kids were happy. When we were able to make time for each other, our relationship was under less stress. I remembered the reasons I had been attracted to Mark in the first place. He was funny, his sharp mind was an enjoyable challenge, not an energy-sapping courtroom. Choosing a life together was enormous fun.

I remember the day we went to Grantham, just over the county border from us. We parked in a supermarket car park and headed to the surprisingly large and elegant parish church, with its chained library and view over the grammar school which Isaac Newton had attended. Since most of my experience of Grantham up to this time was of the congested and charmless one-way system and the retail parks on the edge of town, I was happy to find out that it also had medieval streets, some beautiful old buildings, a well-kept park and a theatre in the guildhall. The main shopping street was less appealing – bargain shops, vape stores and hairdressers – but the town seemed to offer enough possibilities that we stopped for a minute in front of an estate agent opposite the guildhall for a bit of window shopping. Then Mark took my arm.

'Sarah, I feel really strange.' He seemed alarmed and his voice sounded choked.

I put my hand on his shoulder and looked at him. 'What is it? What's happening?'

He did not speak for a few seconds, but continued to stare straight ahead. Then he blinked hard a few times and shook his head slowly.

'I don't know. I felt . . . odd. Not exactly dizzy and not exactly faint, but a bit of both. It felt horrible. Almost like I was going to pass out, but I could still see all right.'

Next door but one to the estate agents, there was a Costa, so I took Mark in there and sat him at a table while I fetched us some coffee and cake. By the time I got back to him, Mark was feeling physically back to normal, but he was worried about what had just happened. We discussed the possibilities, from our limited medical knowledge. Could it have been a small stroke? A heart problem? Or was it just a moment of faintness that would be remedied by a slice of lemon drizzle and a sit-down? Had he forgotten to have breakfast that morning? I was eager to minimize whatever had happened – after all, he had not lost consciousness and there appeared to be no lasting damage. Mark was fit: a good weight, a non-smoker for several years by this time, a non-drinker, a regular runner. You do not run nine miles on Sunday and then have a stroke on Monday, surely? At his last check-up, his blood pressure had been normal. He was fifty-eight. He just did not seem like the type of person who would have serious health problems. And he was fine now. So we went back to the car and drove on to Bourne, a few miles south-east of Grantham.

Bourne was another attractive town, with some fine, early-modern houses and an elegant park with a lido. But, as we were walking back from the park towards the car, Mark stopped suddenly and put his hand on the wall that ran between the pavement and the grass. He said nothing, but, from the expression on his face, I knew it must be happening again. I took his other wrist and found his pulse – regular and strong. As before, the episode lasted less than a minute and Mark was conscious throughout. When it was over, he returned quickly to normal. Mark had two more 'funny turns' that day, each one unpleasant but brief, hard for him to describe and leaving no apparent lasting effect.

If Mark had been suffering with anything common, the next few years might have gone very differently. Within a few weeks, we would have had a diagnosis, a treatment plan, a bunch of leaflets telling us what to expect. There might have been a support group, a referral to a counsellor, a protocol. Instead, we began a period of uncertainty that was to last until his death, four years later. The GP was immediately able to rule out any heart problem, and referred Mark to a neurologist in Leicester. There, he had the first round of tests, traces, examinations and discussions. Were there signs of a stroke? A brain tumour? He was offered various scans, of increasing resolution and complexity. Throughout this period, Mark was having more and more frequent 'events' – sometimes more than forty a day. We got used to them. He had a twenty-four-hour electroencephalogram, an EEG, that involved covering his head in little electrodes which left glue in his hair. With all the wires coming from his scalp, his head looked like a multicoloured teasel. Considering the results of his EEG, the neurologist told Mark that he seemed to be suffering from mild epilepsy. Adult-onset epilepsy is not uncommon. There were drugs that would be able to control his seizures, and he would get better. He would have to stop driving until he had been seizure-free for a year or so, but we could live with that. He began taking epilepsy-control drugs, and, after a few weeks of experimenting to find the right combination of drugs in the right doses, his seizures stopped. Mark joined the Epilepsy Society, I took over all the driving and, for a while, life was normal again.

Six months later, he had another MRI scan on his brain; despite the seizures having mostly stopped, it showed that the area of damage in his brain had expanded, and the damage looked a bit worse. It looked like, rather than the seizures causing brain damage, brain damage was causing seizures, which meant that something else was causing the brain damage. His consultant wondered whether this might be autoimmune encephalitis, and tested Mark's blood for the antibodies most commonly associated with the disease. When those tests all came back negative, she decided to refer him to colleagues – first within Leicester hospitals, then further afield, to Nottingham and then to Oxford, where he met Dr Isabel Maria Leite, who became his consultant and our friend for the rest of his life.

For a few years, we did nothing to advance our new life plan. We worked. We saved up. I bought a notebook with a pattern of butterflies and dandelions on the front. One evening, we left the children with a babysitter, walked down to the Anne of Cleves pub and held the first of our own little strategy meetings. I headed one page *Things Mark might do* and another *Things Sarah might do*. Then I added pages for *Where we might live*, *How much money we will need*, and a more abstract *Things I want in my life* page for each of us. Mark's list of things he might do mostly built on his academic skills and his previous career as a journalist: he could be a proof-reader, an academic editor, a tutor. He could provide or check commercial copy. But he was also keen to investigate the possibility of setting up some kind of business, perhaps as a social enterprise, and probably related to his interest in sustainably produced, locally sourced food. Perhaps it was his Polish heritage, or perhaps it was just that he loved strong, savoury foods, but he had always taken a particular interest in cured meats. At the bottom of his list, he wrote = *SALAMIS?*

The challenge of sourcing organic meat, experimenting with herbs and spices, researching drying periods – he loved all that. He started producing in a small way, making salamis to order for friends, neighbours and colleagues. He ordered equipment and supplies; he befriended a local couple who bred organic, rare-breed pigs and bought his meat from them. He mixed up new recipes, and I often came home to find the kitchen full of slithery tubes of meat, waiting to be hung out to dry.

The problem was that our house had nowhere very sensible to dry the sausages, a process that takes two to three weeks. Our garage was integral to the house. Even though he installed a drying rack on the garage ceiling and bought a second-hand fridge to keep his supplies in (leading to a *Lord of the Flies* moment when Rachel went out to the garage to get some more milk and found half a pig's head in the fridge), the smell of drying pork permeated the house: sweet, cloying, nasty. The kids and I found the stink during the first few days of hanging up a new batch to be quite nauseating. Mark did not seem to notice or mind the stench as much. Maybe that should have worried us.

Mark was a foodie. When he talked about his childhood memories, or told me stories about his long cycle tours across Europe, camping on the way, being gone for months at a time, he was hazy on the names of people he had met or towns he had passed through, but could often recall exactly the meal that he had eaten in any location – grilled sardines at a village in Portugal, jugged hare in northern Italy. He remembered his uncle's duck soup, produced for a family dinner when he was only nine or ten years old. He loved recipes – the more complex and challenging, the better. For our big family Christmases, he liked to find something complicated that would take days to prepare – making a marinade, a stock, a sauce. The kind of recipe where each component needs to be prepared fussily before it can be added, and with an ingredients list so long it would need a second piece of paper.

Our first trip away together, back when we were living in Wales, was for two nights in a tiny garden house in the woods, in the Forest of Dean. The house had a living room and kitchen downstairs, and a bedroom and bathroom upstairs. It was properly Hansel and Gretel, almost hidden by trees, and you could watch the deer while sitting on the sofa with a cup of tea. On our way there, we stopped at Waitrose in Monmouth to buy stuff for our meals and extra treats. We bought Monsoon Malabar coffee, made by exposing the coffee beans to the moist monsoon winds. I had never had it before and it is still my favourite. Mark said he would make a Spanish squid stew that night, another first for me. I wondered if he was showing off a bit, because we were at that stage in our relationship where we were demonstrating all our special features, fanning our tails at each other and fluffing our wings. The squid stew is simple: onion, garlic, cumin, red wine, tomatoes and squid. The trick is to cook the squid for a really long time. Squid, Mark told me, needs to be cooked either very quickly or for ages and ages. Anything in between and you might as well chew a condom. Maybe it was the romance of the forest and the thrill of a new relationship, but I thought the stew was about the most delicious thing I had ever tasted. Full flavours from the wine, garlic and tomato given a rich toastiness by the cumin, and all set off by the mild, inky bitterness of the squid. Beautiful. But I was wrong to think that the squid stew was a special party piece. It turned out to be a dish from Mark's regular repertoire and, in due course, part of the team of workhorse family dinners that everyone enjoyed. We ate it maybe once every couple of months.

The squid stew was also the canary in the coal mine when Mark's sense of smell and taste began to fail, years later. He made the stew as he had done scores of times before. It was the kind of familiar everyday cooking that needs no recipe, but this time something was wrong.

'I hope it's OK,' said Mark. 'I think this garlic must be very old because it doesn't taste of anything at all. I put in almost a whole bulb and you still can't really taste it.'

I took a mouthful and nearly exploded. It was ridiculously,

overpoweringly garlicky. Even I, a committed garlicophile, found it close to inedible, and little Greg looked wide-eyed and distraught, as though he had bitten into a marshmallow and found a pickled onion inside. Only Mark was placidly munching through it like nothing was the matter. To him, it neither tasted nor smelled garlicky.

The absence of a sense of smell is called anosmia. Smell is so closely related to taste that to lose one's sense of smell is also effectively to lose most of the sensitivity and subtlety of one's sense of taste. Most people over sixty have a measurable degree of loss to their sense of taste and smell, but anosmia can also be congenital or come on suddenly or gradually as a result of trauma, illness or for apparently no reason at all. As children, we used to ask each other, 'Would you rather be blind of deaf?' Deaf, I thought, though it was not an easy choice. We never gave one another the option of losing a sense of smell because, I assume, we thought it would not be a big deal. But, as many who have suffered anosmia testify, their loss has been profound. They speak of their isolation. Bee Wilson, the journalist, described in an essay the great grief and disorientation she experienced after losing her sense of smell. A fellow anosmic told her, 'With smell, when breathing in, the world comes inside us. Without smell, when I see things, they just stay where they are. They are nothing to do with me.' Wilson mourns the disappearance of smells that formerly differentiated the seasons for her – the sticky tarmac of urban summers, burning leaves in autumn suburbs, the combined scents of mince pies, oranges and pine resin that evoke the living room at Christmas. Now, the fresh, green joy of spring is lost to her; when her nose shut down, so did her sense of how the world turns.

There are practical problems as well as psychological ones. If you cannot smell good smells, nor can you smell bad ones. How can you be sure if this piece of chicken is still OK, if yesterday's shirt is good for another day, if the washing machine has stopped draining properly or something has died behind the fridge?

While some kinds of anosmia are caused by problems in the nose and throat, other kinds are associated with neurological issues. Anosmia can be a sign of Alzheimer's or Parkinson's disease, for example. The olfactory and gustatory systems that control smell and taste report to several parts of the amygdala and other deep parts of the brain – precisely the areas of Mark's brain where the swelling was first evident and where it was most intense. Smell and taste are part of the limbic system, which is also crucial to emotion, behaviour, motivation and the formation of memory. This might be part of the reason that people find smells are potent evokers of memory, as anyone who has gone back to visit a former place of work will have noticed – the particular and distinctive odours of the corridor and stairwell are immediately transporting.

After the business with the garlic, Mark began to notice more occasions when food did not have the same savour as before. He asked fourteen-year-old Rachel to make a smell test for him at home. She blindfolded him with a scarf and brought a series of redolent spices and substances to his nose: lemon, coffee, ginger, shampoo. For many of them, he could smell something, but struggled to identify it. Some he could not smell at all. A few months later, he was given a more scientific smell test at John Radcliffe Hospital in Oxford. Like Rachel's home-devised version, the standard test for olfactory function feels more like a party game than something medical. The nurse handed Mark what looked like a lidded marker pen. He had to take off the cap, sniff the nib for a few seconds, then choose one of four options from a card. The options included things like grass, leather, vanilla, grapefruit, smoke.

These were my third-chair years. In doctors' offices, there are always chairs for the doctor and the patient, and a third chair for the person accompanying the patient. I sat quietly in the third chair while Mark tried to walk on tiptoe or touch the end of his own nose. I sat in the third chair through many of my mother's mini mental-state tests, in the years leading to her dementia diagnosis, as she tried to count backwards in sevens or tell the doctor the name of the prime minister. It was impossible not to play along silently, remembering the five words the doctor had given her, or the address he had told her at the start of the consultation, which she had to repeat right away, and then again, a few minutes later. I always felt rather pleased with myself for doing well in those tests, even though it was a low bar. It felt good, the same way as 'passing' a blood-pressure check or knowing how to do your ten-year-old child's maths homework feels good: a dopamine hit for cheap.

The smell test, though, I was not confident about. I had discovered, while conducting some informal experiments on my own nose, occasioned by the poor adhesion of my jam labels a few months previously, that it is quite hard to tell apart different flavours of fruit jam if there are no visual cues. Would I be any better at smells than Mark? I think the nurse was used to third-chairs wanting a piece of the action, because I did not even ask – she passed each pen to me after Mark had done his sniff-and-pick. It was harder than I expected, especially the ones that required you to choose between different fruits, or between leather, smoke and wood. I got about 80 per cent of them right. Mark got 20 per cent, a little worse than you would expect to achieve by guessing randomly. When, in the second or third year of his illness, Mark started to suffer from depression, our general thought was that the neurological changes in his head had formed the bleak emotional landscape he now inhabited, but I think that, when he lost his sense of smell, it took much of the pleasure from his life. His dishes were no longer festivals; food was no longer a treat, and he often had little appetite. He lost weight. Meals became, for him, a dutiful refuelling, a matter of getting calories in. Though he still enjoyed coffee, it was a childish appreciation of heat and sweetness now, not savouring the aromatic richness of the Monsoon Malabar.

A bellwether is a sheep with a bell tied round its neck that leads the rest of the flock. Outside shepherding circles, it is more commonly used metaphorically, to mean an early indicator of how things are going – a bellwether state in a US election shows the way things are likely to go nationally on election day. The squid stew was once again the bellwether when Mark's memory began to go. This time, he had made the stew in the normal way, adding cumin and garlic in the quantities he always had, although this was now for our benefit, not his. Anything aromatic was closed to him – his tastes had narrowed to the blunt instruments of salt, sweet, sour, hot. He added the generous half-bottle of wine that this stew needs and let it simmer for a couple of hours. But, as he served it, he seemed concerned.

'It doesn't look right.'

It did not. Something was off. It took me a moment to work it out. It looked wrong and felt wrong – too dark, too thin. The wine, cumin, garlic were all pungently present, but . . .

'The tomatoes,' I said.

Mark looked puzzled. 'Does it normally have tomatoes?'

The stew was edible, though not as rich and delicious as usual. But the bad taste in my mouth had quite another origin. His symptoms so far had all seemed rather hard-edged and specific – seizures, feeling cold, spasms in his feet. But forgetting things was a new one, and forgetting an old and favourite recipe was most out of character.

There had been a few other things. Mark told me that he had spent several minutes trying to remember whether his mother, who had died six years before, was still alive. He had been briefly flummoxed by the mechanics of plugging in the car seat belt. A couple of weeks before this incident, he had blanked on the name of my closest friend. Somebody had called when I was at work, he told me. It was that woman I see quite often, blonde hair, plays football, works for the

Environment Agency. Whatshername. It was no problem for me to recognize Diane from the description. He clearly knew who she was and had remembered to give me the message, but he was disturbed that the name he wanted was not there. I made light of it. We all forget names sometimes. I am always calling the kids by each other's name, or even by the name of my brother or sister, or an old friend from university. My dad once – famously, in our family – called my brother 'Dave', which was not the name of any family member or any of his close friends.

The night of the bellwether stew, I lay awake in bed, wondering whether the absent tomatoes, the lost names, were something or nothing. With no diagnosis, I did not know what to expect of Mark's condition. He seemed less worried than I was, unless he was trying to be optimistic, which would be in character. Was his mild forgetfulness enough to be called a symptom? If it was a symptom, what did it mean? While Mark slept, I sidled out of bed and shuffled into my slippers. Wrapping myself in a dressing gown, I went downstairs and switched on the computer to send a message to Mark's consultant. I summarized his current state, and my concerns:

Forgive me writing on his behalf – he has rather less initiative that formerly, so I am taking over that role, though not always with his knowledge. I will tell him I have contacted you, but not everything I have said, in case it upsets him. I don't think he realizes that his intellectual function has declined, and that would depress him hugely.

I do need to make plans for Mark's future, though, so it would be useful to find out whether his state of mind and/or his memory is likely to improve, or get worse, or stay about the same, so that we can get used to the idea and sort out plans for the future, though I understand that the future, in Mark's case, might be difficult or impossible to predict.

6

COMPASSION IN THE MIDDLE PALAEOLITHIC

A popular meme in my Facebook feed is a quotation purportedly from Margaret Mead, the anthropologist. Mead is quoted as having said that the earliest indication of 'civilization', itself a vexed term, is a human femur with a healed fracture. In a state of nature, a fractured femur would lead inevitably to death; the fact that this break has healed shows that somebody else was taking care of the injured person for long enough that they were able to regain their mobility. This is the origin of compassion, and marks out what makes us human.

The meme is a factoid; there is no evidence that Margaret Mead ever made this remark. It is misleading both about the natural course of events, because animals do sometimes heal from serious fractures, and about how Mead and other anthropologists of her time defined civilization, usually around social complexity, redistribution of wealth and so on. The quotation is probably made up, but there is an important and attractive truth in it, which is that caring for people who cannot apparently offer a reciprocal material benefit to us is indicative of a society in which empathy is a significant driver of doing the right thing.

Archaeologists who study death spend a lot of time thinking about, and examining, human bones. The long bones in our body have a proximal and a distal end, the proximal end being the one closest to the main body, and the distal end further away. My research interests are in the proximal past, the periods nearest to us now, but many of my colleagues are fascinated by the distal end – the earliest modern humans, and the hominins that came before them. Palaeolithic archaeologists tend to have strong views about the question of what makes us human, and some reject it altogether as a meaningless categorization. For others, however, the answer is compassion. Selfless behaviour exists among other animals, including apes and elephants. I love one account of how an orphaned baby chimpanzee was adopted by an unrelated twelve-year-old male, who carried the baby on his back and brought it into his nest at night. But caring behaviour that involves an element of cost to the individual seems to be more sustained and widespread among humans than other animals. From as early as the Middle Palaeolithic, pre-modern hominins were displaying behaviour that could be considered compassionate. Much of the evidence for this is inferred from the remains of individuals who had conditions that would have either temporarily or permanently affected their ability to take care of their own material needs. In most animal groups, the usual fate of individuals who suffered a serious fracture, for example, and became unable to hunt for themselves or run away from predators, would be death.

In my part of the archaeological record, the proximal end, evidence of care for the unrelated old, the sick, the disabled, for children and even animals is widespread. But there are some affecting and poignant examples from the deep past too. Between 60,000 and 80,000 years ago, a middle-aged Neanderthal man was buried, probably deliberately, in Shanidar Cave, in northern Iraq. The site is famous because it contains the remains of several Neanderthals and their tools, but also because of this man, Shanidar 1. During his life, he suffered multiple fractures across his body, including a break in his upper right arm, following which his entire arm became atrophied and would have withered. It is possible that he lost his lower arm and hand altogether. Additionally, injuries to his head probably left him blind in one eye. He might also have had a severe degree of hearing loss. Those injuries happened in his adolescence, and yet he did not die until he was thirty-five to forty-five years old. To have survived so long, many Palaeolithic archaeologists have argued, Shanidar 1 must have been fed and supported by his group, and that, the archaeologists say, is the dawn of compassion. Shanidar 1 is not alone. It is estimated that up to 60 per cent of Neanderthal individuals whose bones show trauma, also show healing. Given that it takes around four to six weeks for a broken bone to heal, that means support or help from others for a sustained period. Even more remarkable than evidence of care-giving through a period of reduced fitness are the cases in which we can infer care and compassion even though the individual was not going to recover. There are cases of adults without teeth, whose smoothed-over tooth sockets show that they survived even though they would have struggled with the meat-based diet which, it is thought, provided Neanderthals with most of their calories. Was somebody else chewing their food for them? And there are cases of people whose disabilities were congenital or permanent, such as the teenager known as Romito 2, found in southern Italy, who had a congenital form of dwarfism.

The evidential value of disability or trauma for the existence of a compassionate society is interesting, but I think there could be other approaches too. It is hard to find archaeological accounts of disability that are not about stigma or compassion. I have been looking for anything that uses archaeological evidence to examine what the experience of having a disabled body might have been in the past, but so far with meagre success. I ask myself, Would a monumental structure still inspire awe in somebody who could not see? How would a mighty processional way appear to somebody who could not walk, or an elaborate feast to somebody who could not lift food to their own lips?

In the summer of 2014, we went on holiday to Pembrokeshire. Rachel had gone to a music festival with her friends, so it was just Mark and me and the boys, in a rental house about half a mile from the beach. When I was a kid, we used to go on caravan holidays to Pembrokeshire, and, as I became older, I used to hitchhike there from university exclusively to gaze out to sea and feel misunderstood. The first time I went on holiday with a boyfriend, it was to camp behind the beach at Newgale Sands. My summer job at Castell Henllys, in the north of the county, when I was eighteen, was the first time I encountered archaeology. During the

Lampeter years, weekend trips to explore the Preseli Hills and the coastal villages were favourite jaunts for me. It was good to go back.

Despite good days by the sea, and boat trips to see the sea birds, we were snappish with each other that summer. Mark's mood was dark; he was annoyed with me and the children, and with himself: he said more than once that we would be better off without him. But he liked the cottage we had rented, and looking for fossils among the shale that had fallen from the cliffs. Mark loved fossils. As a child, he had taken all his clothes out from his chest of drawers and stuffed them under the bed to make a proper place to lay out the collection he had accumulated from quarry sites around Essex, escorted on the bus by his long-suffering mother. Our sons, Adam and Greg, were still young enough that year to find a day out with a picnic exciting, so we took long walks along the coastal path. The footpath hugs the cliff edge, through fields, sprawls of gorse and sheep-cropped grass. Every mile or so, another small stream opens into the sea, and the path winds down to a footbridge or a few stepping stones, and then steeply back up to the clifftop. Climbs are short but sharp, and I felt out of breath and leg-achy on the ascents. Mark was plainly also struggling. He told me his legs felt weak, that he could not lift them properly: could it be something to do with his illness? I thought not. My legs felt tired too, I told him. We were just out of shape. Mark had not been running regularly for about a year, not only because he was depressed and listless, but also because he found that running often induced more seizures, which were no longer well controlled by the drugs. I thought he was pathologizing something that was only unfitness. His regular medical checks involved monitoring his muscle tone and getting him to perform a series of physical tasks: heel-to-toe walking, demonstrating the range of motion in his arms, legs, hands and feet. Could he use his body symmetrically? Could he touch his nose with his finger? None of those tests had shown any physical problem. Despite his misgivings, Mark did not fall on the coast path. He managed our walks without incident and, complacently, I assumed I had been right: we both just needed to do more jogging.

I remembered his worry about his legs though, about four months later, on our way back from the chicken farm, down Sandy Lane. What we called the chicken farm was in reality just a smallholding with a few hens, on the edge of Great Dalby, two and a half miles from our house, where we used to buy eggs. To walk there and back was an easy afternoon stroll down a quiet, rural lane lined with ash trees and across a disused airfield. I often did it on my own, but, the day after his birthday, a Saturday at the end of November, Mark decided to come with me. I remember enjoying the walk, filling our empty egg boxes, replacing them in the backpack and setting off home. Halfway down Sandy Lane, Mark curved away from me towards the hedge on the right-hand side of the road.

'Where are you going?'

'I don't mean to be going anywhere. I'm not doing this on purpose. For some reason, I'm finding it hard to walk in a straight line.'

I pulled him back to the middle of the lane, but the same thing happened again as soon as I let go of his arm. This time, when I pulled him back, I kept my arm around his waist and held him close to me so that we could walk together. As we went on, it took more and more strength, first to resist him pulling me over to the right, and then to help support his weight as his legs began to give way beneath him. He was getting weaker, and his feet were starting to drag. For the last quarter mile, he was barely able to stand, and had next to no control over his direction. We must have looked drunk, staggering haphazardly back into Melton. When we finally got home, he dropped into his armchair, exhausted and frightened by what had happened to his body. This was clearly more than just being out of shape.

Next morning, he seemed back to normal, and decided to try a short run. I was worried that, if he lost control of his body again, he could fall, or that he would be powerless if his legs decided to take him into the road and in front of passing cars, so I put on my running shoes and went with him. We had barely reached the end of our cul-de-sac and turned onto the road when he began again to veer to the right, and found that he could not reliably pick up his feet high enough not to trip, so we abandoned the run and I helped him home, before it got any worse. That turned out to be the last time he put on running shoes. Later, he would ask me to get rid of them, because seeing them in his wardrobe whenever he went to get out a jumper was too depressing.

Mark's next brain scan, the following month, showed that

the 'florid and extensive' inflammation that was slowly colonizing his brain had crossed the pons, literally the bridge, from the midbrain to the medulla, and onwards down his spinal cord. The brain stem and spinal cord were now both affected by whatever it was. His whole central nervous system. The astonishing, complex and efficient circuitry that let Mark walk, run, jump, dance, embrace his children, take his partner's hand, type, write, chop vegetables, dig in the garden – all those things – had started to go wrong. Signals were not always getting through, or not reliably, not every time. Or one side of his body worked properly, but the other did not; his movements became asymmetrical. The brainstem is also where the regulation of crucial life-sustaining functions takes place. If it did not limit itself, the damage would eventually stop him from eating, his lungs from breathing, his heart from beating.

I imagined the inflammation like a kind of spreading rot, pushing its malevolent fingers into every corner of Mark's brain and now reaching out, down his body, first his right side, then his left, his bowels and his bladder, his skin, his senses, his happiness. As the disease moved on, so Mark's symptoms also worsened, to include new sensations caused by the spinal-cord damage – terrible itching over the skin of his back, twitching in his feet that caused pain and could not be stopped.

Some effects came and went. I remember a few weeks when Mark was freezing cold all the time. He would sit inside with his coat and woolly hat on, blankets piled over him, the central heating on all the time, while the rest of us sweltered in T-shirts. And then after a couple of months it went away, and his temperature regulation returned to normal. Another time, he was taken over by the compulsion to shout obscenities in quiet or formal situations, like the library, or in a meeting. Once, it was so bad he had to put his hand over his mouth and leave the room. Then that passed too. I suppose the wave of damage passed through a particular place in his brain and moved on. But the territory it passed over did not always regenerate.

7

ST RICHARD OF THE CAR PARK

Ironically, as things were falling apart in my home and family life, life at work was going swimmingly. I had successfully put together a grant proposal for nearly a million pounds to lead an interdisciplinary research project. The project was all about what happened to the bodies of executed criminals in Britain, especially in the period between the 1752 Murder Act and the 1832 Anatomy Act, when the bodies of those executed for murder could not be buried in the normal way, but had to be sent to the anatomists for dissection or suspended in gibbets to decay slowly over months or years. I had assembled a team including a medical historian, a crime historian, a folklorist, a philosopher, an archaeologist and a literary scholar, as well as a bunch of junior researchers, and we were proceeding with remarkable energy and success, churning out books and articles, finding terrific new material and new ways to interpret it. Because the grant came on top of a solid few years of weighty publications and a full teaching load, the university promoted me to a chair, which meant better pay and getting to use the title Professor. At the same time, however, another archaeological event in Leicester far outshone my project in terms of public appeal. Some of my colleagues, excavating a car park in the city centre in the hope of finding out more about the old Franciscan friary, had made a remarkable discovery. I remember coming into the department one summer morning in 2012 to be pulled quickly into my friend Deirdre's office.

'Have you heard?' Deirdre was ready to explode with news. 'They've found Richard III!'

The possibility that Richard III could have been buried in the Greyfriars chapel had been discussed for years, and provided a sweetener for funding and publicity. Neither I nor any of my colleagues thought privately that any such discovery was very likely, but it was a nice story, and the university had made a press release around the connection.

'Really? And was he . . . ?' I mimed a Shakespearian hump.

'*Yes!*' Deirdre's eyes widened even further. 'It looks like it. But we're not to tell anyone at all. And the Richard III Society are disappointed about the hump, because they're quite invested in him being kind of buff, but we're not taking instructions from them. The university intends to keep very tight control over who knows what and when.'

It seemed that the Richard III Society had scored something of an own goal when the project they had hoped would confirm that Richard's disfigurements were only Tudor propaganda instead provided proof that he did indeed have a spinal condition.

So, it was not until the following February, when the lab and historical work was complete, that the university went public with the news, and the country – at times it seemed like the whole world – came down with Richard fever.

I had not been part of the Richard III project, but I did have some relevant expertise, and there were suddenly a million demands on the core team, so I was co-opted to give a few talks at schools and local history societies, and to represent the university on the committee for arranging the material details of the reinterment, which was now to be an extravaganza of Ricardian pomp, televised around the world. The theatricality culminated in a week of ceremony and events leading up to and away from the reinterment of the unlucky king's remains on Thursday, 26 March 2015. The Sunday before, Mark and the boys accompanied me to a ceremony to commemorate the departure from the university premises of what were being treated for all purposes as holy relics. The committee I was on included representatives from the university, the city, the cathedral and the Richard III Society. I had given enough talks, including a couple at the cathedral, and participated in enough meetings that I knew several of the diocesan staff and had met a few members of the Richard III Society, a clutch of free-range eggs if ever there was one. The university team were mostly personal chums, so it was enjoyable that Sunday morning to gossip with friends and acquaintances, while holding a plastic cup of Pinot Grigio and keeping a nervous eye on the boys in the hope that they were not eating all the crisps.

Few of his former colleagues at the university were aware that Mark was unwell. He was keen to keep it that way, but a stand-up reception was a challenge. By the spring of 2015, walking a few hundred metres had become hard, and being on his feet for any length of time was something he tried to avoid. I looked up from talking to Turi, the geneticist on the project, and could not see Mark in the hall. Adam and Greg had teamed up with a couple of girls about their age, and the four of them were giggling by the windows. Greg was on all fours under a table. I excused myself to Turi and scurried over to them.

'Have you seen Dad?'

'Um, no. He might be having a look at the coffin?'

Richard III's coffin was resting on trestles in the foyer of the building, waiting to begin its ceremonial journey away from the university. Many of the guests had already taken the opportunity to touch it, either overtly, or a surreptitious brush, scratching an itch for an authentic and tangible encounter with history. I know I stroked the coffin when I came past it. I think Adam did too. Half a dozen people were milling around it now, but none of them was Mark. He will be looking for somewhere to sit down, I thought, and headed to the cloakroom. Sure enough, there he was, sitting on a plastic chair, behind a rack of coats, looking tetchy.

'You're missing the fun. Shall we try to go back to the hall? I can bring the chair.'

'I don't want to be the only one sitting down, looking like a bloody cripple. I can manage.'

Holding my arm, Mark walked slowly back to the hall in time for the first of the day's many speeches. He half-leaned, half-sat on one of the long tables at the side of the room. The next stage was harder, though. We were herded into groups and then each group was led out of the building and made to line up in rows flanking the doors to the building, through which the coffin eventually came, followed by more speeches and readings. During this process, Mark, the two boys and I became separated. I was in a row to the left of the door, with Greg a little in front of me. I could not see Adam or Mark, and I was worried. The whole outdoor part of the ceremony took more than forty-five minutes. There was no way that Mark could stand unsupported all that time. Where was he? I hoped he was all right, and not missing the event we had come for. We stood patiently and sombrely through a load of dutifully multifaith readings and some lugubrious funerary theatre, as a couple of dozen team members laid white roses on a velvet cushion. I have been looking at the recording of the ceremony that is still available on YouTube. I can see Greg easily, standing just behind the chaplain. I know where I was, just out of shot. Mark told me later that he was able to lean on a wall and made it through the ceremony without collapsing, but I could not see him in the video until, after some scrutiny, Adam spotted the top of his father's head in the early part of the recording. He was standing behind me, quite close, but out of my sight. Greg remembers the occasion well. He says he was feeling so giggly at the reverent and silent rose-laying part that he had to bite the inside of his cheek to keep from laughing aloud.

Four days later, I was in a numbered seat in St Martin's Cathedral for the reinterment service. Being only an extra in this carefully choreographed performance, I was not in a prime spot, but had been allocated a place behind a screen in a chapel near the south door, in front of which a row of TV camera operators had set up, so I could not see anything much – though, if I leaned to the left a bit, I could see the back of Benedict Cumberbatch's head, through a gap between cameramen's bottoms. While I quite enjoyed being part of the fuss, getting to dress up and look for myself on TV afterwards (unsuccessfully), I also felt a little embarrassed to have been complicit in this pompous mummery. Some of my colleagues had started privately referring to the late king as 'St Richard', and certainly his devotees had something of the fanatical cult about them. It was ludicrous, really. A man dead for more than five hundred years: we none of us knew him. But here we were, saying prayers for him, honouring him with our time, our presence, lining the streets. I found out later that the route the coffin took through Leicester was decorated with 5,929 white roses, made by local school-children, each of which represented one of the Leicestershire people who go missing each year. That number seemed shock-ingly high, so I checked it. The charity Missing People says that, in the whole of the UK, 176,000 people per year are reported missing to the police, so 5,929 is a reasonable figure for one county. Most of them are found within a few days, but between 2 per cent and 5 per cent stay missing for more than a week, and some of them are never found. So, while a long-dead man, of contested reputation, who was not missing but merely misplaced, gets all this hoo-ha and our long faces and moments of silence, each missing person, with a living family and anguished friends, gets a paper flower. Looked at like that, it was grotesque. It is surely not ethical that deference to monarchy, or historical romanticism, trumps living emotional pain. Nobody there was returning to a home which still had Richard's jacket hanging on a peg in the hall; none of the congregation was weeping alone at night for him. The ostentatious sentiment poured into Richard III's reburial was disproportionate. What about all the quiet losses, the ordinary grief? What about the people who were not kings, but no less loved, no less admired, and a good deal more missed?

Fourteen months later, I was back for a much smaller, quieter ceremony, a few metres from the cathedral, in the guildhall next door. This time, we were remembering Mark.

While he had enjoyed the beauty of the Welsh coast, what Mark really wanted was the kind of warmth and sunshine you can only be sure of, if you live in Britain, by going abroad. For the summer after our Wales trip, he wanted a holiday that would lift his mood and warm his cold limbs. Our trip would be a light that he could drag himself towards through the dark days of uncertainty and the chill of our relationship. Would this holiday still be possible? How would he feel in the heat? In February, when we booked our week in Corfu, Mark was still able, with his frame, to walk a mile or more. By the time we went, in July, he needed a wheelchair to go further than two or three steps. I was worried that we would struggle to get on and off the plane, that the apartment might be hard to access in his chair, that going away would be more stressful than staying home, but Mark was positive and optimistic about the trip. When I suggested we think about cancelling or going somewhere closer, he was emphatic: 'This might be my last chance to go abroad. Even if it's hard, let's try and find a way.'

I need not have worried. I am glad Mark got to have his week in the sun. He was happy then. And he was right: it was his last trip abroad, and his last holiday.

We had a two-bed apartment in a holiday complex on a sheltered bay. There was a narrow, gravelly beach, edged with muddy banks of samphire on the north side and a few boat sheds on the south. The complex had a pool, a garden of spiky grass and some dogged and dusty succulents, a café, and a small shop selling ice cream and swimming trunks. We bought the children each a cheap, colourful lilo, and they spent their days swimming and paddling their inflatables round the bay. I was up first every morning to walk down the road to the supermarket and bakery for supplies, then back to help Mark get up, washed and dressed. After breakfast was cleared away, I was free most of the day to read, swim and stare into space. Apart from a couple of trips to nearby restaurants in the evenings, we did not leave the resort. Mark slept a great deal, and ate little, but he was happy to sit under the pergola by the pool, drinking coffee and reading day-old newspapers. Once, he got into the pool, craving the feel of water on his skin. I held him up and let the water take his weight, but getting him out again took both boys and me, all hauling and pushing as though we were trying to land a walrus – an exercise in indignity that he chose not to repeat. Moreover, he felt unsafe in the pool, aware that he was wholly dependent on me supporting him.

He was in a position of vulnerability that was new to him, and hard to accommodate.

I think there is a gender difference, here. We women are used to our bodies not being entirely in our control. We are always having to go to the doctor's – for smear tests and mammograms, for contraception, for pregnancies (both the ones we wanted and the ones we did not). We are used to resigning our bodies to the care of others, to being told that we are weak, leaky, prone to breaking down or malfunctioning, that we require intervention. Men are the ones who, in my experience, cope badly with any bodily failure. Before he was ill, Mark was confident in his physicality – a champion hurdler in his youth, a cyclist and a runner into middle age. His body had never let him down before.

A few weeks after we got back from Corfu, Dr Leite suggested that Mark start a course of high-dose steroids. These should reduce the inflammation in his brain, she said, and, with luck, subdue his symptoms at the same time. High-dose steroids have serious side effects and are not usually recommended for long-term use. They are also difficult to stop taking, so this had not been a first-line treatment for Mark. And, however effective they might be, they were treating only the inflammation and not the cause of the inflammation, which remained elusive. Initially, the results were miraculous. Three days into his new regime, I let myself into the house after work and heard Mark shout, 'Wait there!'

A moment later, he came out of the kitchen and walked up the hall towards me, grinning.

'Look at this!' He was holding his hands up to show he had no walking frame up his sleeve, no concealed wheelchair. We hugged each other. For the first time in months, I was standing with my arms around Mark as an equal participant in the embrace, not supporting his weight.

We were exuberantly happy for a few days, but then the effects of the steroids, even in nuclear doses, began to wane. We reinstated the frame, and the chair. We had seen false dawns like this before. Three days after his first plasma exchange, the previous year, we went to a country park with our kids and my brother Ben's family. Mark was like he used to be. He was able to walk around the lakes and play with the children. No less miraculous was the transformation in his mood. He was joking with my sister-in-law, he was talkative and happy, paying attention to the children. In the playground, he pushed half a dozen wriggling, squealing children on the giant swing. But, two days later, he was back in the squashy orange armchair which had become his customary spot, struggling to walk or to feel anything but bleak and empty.

The happy man, the joker, the swinger of children, the adventurer, the flirt – he was easy to love. But the silent man, the irritable man, the cynic, the picker of fights, the man whose triumphs were receding and whose future was crumbling – not so much. Did I still love him? I suppose I did, underneath the frustration. But that hardly seemed relevant, by then. My love was too weak to sustain us through those days. I felt sorry for his pain, for his evident unhappiness, but I could not easily love him when he was caustic and wounding to the children. Against such anger, there was only the feeling that I was doing my duty. There was only trying to do the right thing.

I wish I had known, though, what was the right thing to do. Even with hindsight, I do not know how I should have been. I am not sure that the right thing for Mark would have been the right thing for the children. My solution was to keep them separate as much as I was able. I took the kids for walks in all weathers, forcing them into raincoats and woolly hats, jollying through their protests, or we went to visit friends. I encouraged Mark to make himself comfortable somewhere he would have the room to himself. I brought him cups of tea in bed while he read, and I coaxed the children to the telly when he was sitting in the kitchen, so that they would not run around and crash into him, or say something that would earn them a harsh response and lead to tears, shouting, slammed doors and hurt feelings. We ate meals together, as we always had done, but often now these were tense or bad-tempered occasions. Mark would sometimes ridicule the children's friends or their interests, or mimic Adam's noisy chewing with a grotesque pantomime of animal feeding. I fussed around, on a hair trigger for any subject arising that might end in crying or yelling. If I could anticipate the way a conversation might go, I could try to head it off early. Could I treat the unexploded comment or the hurtful burlesque as though Dad had meant it as a joke, though we all knew he had not? Should I take sides? I wish I had known how to get this right. I wish this nasty man had not decided to occupy Mark.

8

PROBLEMATIC STUFF IN THE IRON AGE

Within a week of Mark's death, I had disposed of most of his clothes. It was not hard. Mark had few personal possessions and was not emotionally invested in any of them. I put aside a couple of good coats for my nephews; everything else went to the charity shop. For other people, sorting out a dead person's stuff can be much harder, both emotionally and logistically. Undoubtedly, the task of clearing his stuff was made easier because he did not have very much of it – apart from books, which I mostly kept. In part, this was because we had moved house just a few months before, an event which prompted a severe edit of all our belongings.

I came across a feature in the paper a few weeks ago about the new vogue for *döstädning* – 'death cleaning', in Swedish. The practice was championed by Margareta Magnusson in response to her experience of clearing out the homes of her friends and relatives who had died. She wanted to spare her children the hassle and emotional pain of dealing with all her hoarded stuff, or finding, in old letters, journals and photographs, personal details they would rather not know. A 'death clean' is a thorough sort-out in advance. I can see the benefits and should probably crack on with it myself. In the loft, I have five boxes of photos and slides from my mother's house, as yet unsorted. Some I will want to keep: pictures of my sister, brother and me when we were little, for example, and a set of double-exposed pictures from 1965, in which my parents' wedding photos, with them looking clueless and young, are superimposed on the pictures of their graduation. Whoever took the photographs that eventful summer did not keep track of which films were new and which were ready for developing. But there are also lots of snaps of people I do not recognize and long-ago holidays that nobody now remembers. I ought, at least, to spare my kids the drag of going through all that.

Margareta Magnusson notes that, these days, we tend to have more and more stuff, and it is a problem when the stuff outlasts us. Do we want to stockpile immense warehouses of heirlooms because it is all too significant and sentimental to chuck? I do not. But what can be done with the stuff that was important and meaningful to you? You can't take it with you, the platitude goes, but we archaeologists know that you can. Some of those who died in Europe 2,000 years ago took into their graves not only clothes, jewellery, tools, weapons and, in effect, a dinner service, but also their animals, chariots and, disturbingly, possibly even a servant or retainer. The modern-day equivalent would be if I had buried Mark with his old Volvo and maybe the plumber.

But, in some cases, disposing of the possessions of the dead can be very hard. Old theories of bereavement used to focus on how the bereaved detached from the dead and, through a series of stages, got back to normal. These days, specialists in bereavement prefer a model they call 'continuing bonds'. There is no normal to get back to, they say, and relationships continue, even when one of the people in them dies. Instead, we should focus more on accommodating to a new normal. In this process, material things have a role to play, as proxies for the dead person, or as mementoes of them or of a life together. So, new widows sleep in the shirts that still smell like their husband; the decision to take off a wedding ring can be difficult. Sometimes, mundane objects are transformed by associations and timing into vessels brimming with emotional significance and mnemonic power. Young widow Kate Boydell talks in her book about the turned wooden shaving bowl that her late husband used. After his death, she kept it as it had been on the last day of his life, the dried soap still bearing the traces of his shaving brush where it had swirled for the final time. She talks of her anguish when her little child picked up her father's old shaving brush and playfully swept it around the bowl, unwittingly obliterating that ephemeral mark that he had left on the material world.

Archaeologist Lindsey Büster combed the bereavement literature on continuing bonds to help her understand a series of deliberately hidden objects recovered from inside the walls and beneath the floors of late Iron Age roundhouses at the settlement of Broxmouth, in southern Scotland. She thinks that the objects recovered from these unusual contexts might be what she calls 'problematic stuff' – things that are too bound up with the identity of the dead and too emotionally weighty for the everyday use of the living. The Broxmouth artefacts, bone spoons and stone querns, were humdrum things, not valuable treasures or masterpieces of craftsmanship. Their meanings were probably very personal.

On the last day of November 2015, we left our old house in Melton Mowbray and moved into the new one in Grantham. Why, despite Mark's declining health, did we swap our comfortable, modern house in Melton Mowbray for an impractical, characterful Georgian terrace in Grantham? On the face of it, moving house was stupid. It left us with much more work to do, in a town where we knew nobody. It meant a different house, which was not well organized for a person with mobility difficulties and, because it was an old building, would be hard to adapt. It meant a new GP, who knew nothing of Mark's complicated and uncertain history. The first time we met with the new doctor in Grantham, he became quite frustrated with what he thought was our unwillingness to tell him what condition Mark had. He thought we were a pair of confused old fools who had failed to grasp or retain difficult medical language. He would not listen to, or believe, our accounts of Mark's illness, nor would he accept the inconclusive results of his tests and scans. Finally, in frustration at our inability to answer the simple question of what was the matter with Mark, he phoned our old medical practice in Melton, and only then was he was convinced that we did not have a diagnosis. Adam was already at school in Grantham, anticipating our house move, so he would be fine. But it meant a new school for Greg, only six months before he would be leaving primary school anyway. It meant that Rachel, now away at university, would be returning in her vacations to a house that had never been her home, in a town many miles away from all her friends, with only a limited bus service. And it meant, I was under no illusions, that I would need to take care of all the practicalities on my own, because Mark could barely move.

Why did we do it? Mainly, we moved because it was essential to Mark's mental well-being that he have some hope of recovery. We were trying, even with each other, to pretend that our story was going to have the happy ending we had previously drafted. He wanted the large garden and the outbuildings so that he could make salami and live the life we had planned together a few years earlier. I think I knew, even when we bought the house, that he was unlikely ever to use the outbuilding to dry salamis; I knew he would never be able to push a lawnmower or paint the ceilings. I suspected that the stairs would soon prove impossible for him. But we went ahead anyway. We were not about to kick over the sandcastle of his dreams. Was our obstinate refusal to acknowledge a hopeless reality pathetic or admirable? I am still not sure. When the looming and likely future looks as savage and barren as Mark's did then, there is something to be said for flat denial.

We had, moreover, started down this road. Adam had already started secondary school in Grantham because we were planning to move there. We had agreed a sale of our Melton house from which it felt rude to backtrack, leaving the purchasers stranded and breaking a chain.

Finally, we did not know what else to do. Moving house

was at least doing something purposeful – and it felt good, in the face of adversity, to have a project, with its own deadlines and to-do lists. Before Adam was born, I'd had a miscarriage in the second trimester of my pregnancy. There was nothing to be done. I had to accept the disappointment and grief and try again; but I am extremely bad at patient waiting. Doing nothing while the days passed made me feel worse. I remember coming back from the hospital after the D and C and sorting out all our photos into albums. It did not get us a baby, but I felt something had been achieved at a time when failure was the theme of my life. Sorting photos was a good way to scratch my itch for action; moving house was not.

A few weeks before, when we were looking at places we might live, Mark had been able to walk around houses unaided, even going upstairs and into the garden, though he could not manage more than a couple of visits in a day. This was the period of the steroids, when things had again seemed possible – a modified normal, for him. But, by the time we completed the purchase of our new house, he could not move more than a couple of steps without a frame.

My good friend Diane, whose marital split the previous year had ended with her moving to a new, smaller house around the corner from her old family home, was worried about how I would cope with the emotional impact of leaving Melton. She came over in the late morning, as we were preparing to leave the old house, expecting to comfort me as I cried. Instead, I thrust a dustpan and brush at her and asked her to give the kitchen a sweep while I hoovered upstairs. I am embarrassed still to think how cursory my cleaning of the house was. I was too preoccupied with simply getting our possessions out and trying to clear up the worst of our mess to give any thought to the emotional challenge of ending our thirteen years in Melton.

We did not finish unloading the van till about eight o'clock that evening, but as we sat eating Chinese takeaway around our newly unpacked table, which had been jammed into the wrong room because it would not fit through the door into the dining room, I let myself feel a little optimism. We had managed it. It was stressful, the place looked like a storage facility and there was still lots to be done, but, even with Mark so weak, we had managed to move house. Maybe we could construct some kind of future here after all.

The new house was the eastern one of a row of three town houses, built sometime between 1815 and 1820. It was set well back from the busy A road, down a drive that was permanently shadowed by mature and ivy-covered trees. The drive was damp and mossy, treacherous in wet weather, and the tarmac was potholed and cracked, colonized by grass and tenacious little buddleias. A narrow front lawn, mostly moss, ran parallel to the drive, with snowberries and lilacs encroaching around the edges. A flight of three steep stone steps led to a narrow terrace in front of the house. Inside, the rooms were high ceilinged and formerly elegant, though made ugly by shiny yellow paint over textured wallpaper, and grubby beige carpet. There was a living room at the front and another at the back, both of which felt cavernously high, and an oddly shaped kitchen, built into a rear extension, all alcoves and vestigial bits of wall, with a pantry cupboard biting a chunk out of the corner. Between the hall and the kitchen was a small room with doors on both long walls and a window with crumbling plaster falling from the reveal. Greg called it the pre-kitchen. When we moved in, the pre-kitchen was as far as we could get our kitchen table. To our consternation, it was too big to go through the door into the actual kitchen, so, for the first few days, it remained half in the pre-kitchen and partly sticking out into the hall, so that we had to edge round it to get through the house. Upstairs were four bedrooms and a bathroom at a slightly lower level, which was accessed from the final curve of the staircase. To leave the bathroom, you had to step up and go through the door onto a wedge-shaped step, below the level of the landing. The bathroom had a bath and a separate shower. The latter was important for Mark, who would not have been able, by then, to step over the side of a bathtub.

The whole place smelled of damp, an aroma that had been semi-successfully masked with lavender Air Wick when we had made our visits prior to buying it. Moss grew on the roof and in the gutters. The chimney was blocked. We could not work out how to operate the central-heating system, which seemed to go on and off at the most erratic times. It turned out later that an enigmatic device that had shown up in the bottom of the fitted wardrobe in the boys' bedroom was the remote for the central-heating control; Greg had been using it as a pretend mobile phone. Diane, the friend who had come to console me over leaving Melton, referred to it as 'the Scooby Doo house'. This did not make me feel any better about it. The most pressing problem, after we had managed to fit in all our furniture, was dealing with the damp. I spoke to a builder who specialized in old houses, who advised me to take up the hall carpet, to light a fire in the living room and, when the weather permitted, to keep the doors and windows open. I have been doing all those things for five years now and still have not solved the issue, but taking up the damp beige carpet in the hall, and the surprising layer of roofing felt I found underneath, did reveal a rather lovely floor of limestone slabs, which is probably as old as the house. The builder was a handsome man of about my age, with interesting conversation and a deep knowledge of historical buildings. He made several visits over the next year or so, lingering each time for coffee in the kitchen or on the patio, and he came to occupy more of my imaginative life than he probably expected. At that time, there was something especially appealing to me about a healthy and cultured man, with practical skills and easy conversation. My fantasies were not the erotic ones you might expect a woman of a certain age to indulge in, but centred on a vision of a strong-jawed man putting up curtain rails and sorting out the car. In a confident, manly voice, my imaginary lover would show me which bits of wall needed repointing. A man could have bathed in pheromones with no effect on me at all, but the aroma of Swarfega and white spirit would have made me window putty in his broad and calloused hands. Not that I had the energy, opportunity or inclination for anything improper, but I figured I deserved a bit of a daydream.

9

TERMINUS ANTE QUEM

Archaeological stratigraphy records the sequence of material events in the past, but it gives us a relative, rather than an absolute, chronology. That is to say, it tells us which thing happened before or after which other thing, but it cannot say, 'This thing happened in 426 BC, and this thing in 350 BC.' Because a stratigraphic sequence blows freely in the winds of time, we try to find points to peg it down. Sometimes these are dates derived from scientific analysis – radiocarbon dates or thermoluminescence, for example. Sometimes they are places where we can tie an archaeologically observable event, such as an earthquake or the sacking of a city, to a historically known event. Fixed points might be small or large, closely or more loosely dated, a coin with a year on it or the advent of a new technology. These fixed points give us dates before or after which a particular event must have occurred. For example, a coin dated AD 930 cannot have entered the archaeological record before that date. If such a coin were found in the foundations of a wall, that wall cannot have been built before 930, its *terminus post quem*, literally 'point after which'. If that wall is in turn covered by a layer of burned debris that corresponds to a major fire recorded in the year 1000, that means the wall was completed before then – it cannot be later than 1000. The burned layer provides a *terminus ante quem*, a limit before which the event must have happened. So long as we have a stratigraphical sequence, even if we cannot date each component ('context', in our jargon), given some *termini post* or *ante quem*, we can build a timeline that dates our wall to the period AD 930 to AD 1000. I rarely use the terms *terminus post quem* and *terminus ante quem* myself. I am OK with the Latin. I went to a comprehensive school, but one which had not received the memo that said kids like us should not receive a classical education, so I have a few years of being taught Virgil by scruffy Mr Taylor, whose disintegrating suit jacket was held together by staples. The problem is that I am never entirely sure whether the dates are before/after which a thing *must* have happened or *cannot* have happened. I need the rest of the sentence. I have seen the terms defined both ways in places that ought to know better. I do love archaeological stratigraphy, though. In a world of uncertainty and equifinality, stratigraphy does have a right answer. It is the sudoku of archaeological method.

In organizing the stratigraphy of my own memories, it helps to have some fixed and datable points. We were on the Pembrokeshire coastal path when Mark first felt his legs becoming weak, so that must have been the summer of 2014. I know the dates when we went to Corfu, and therefore that Mark was using a wheelchair most of the time at least by the summer of 2015. Our last Christmas together is another good *terminus ante quem* for me. By December, we were in the new house and Greg was about to start his new school in Grantham. The smelly carpet was still in the hall, because I can remember trying to extract Christmas-tree needles from it.

We had three and a half weeks between moving in and Christmas Day. There were still boxes to unpack, and nowhere to unload our books and CDs until I had arranged for somebody to come and fit shelves in the front room. I needed urgently to find an electrician, a plumber, a roofer, a chimney sweep, a carpenter and a builder. I needed to make the bedrooms habitable.

Even when my relationship with Mark was good, I had valued having my own space when possible. I sleep lightly, and Mark always snored like a road drill. This was on top of the World Service going all night. He would often drop off while reading, too, so the bedside light would stay on. None of this appeared to affect his ability to sleep long and deeply, but, for me, it was about as restful as sleeping in a bus station. In the Melton house, I had developed a routine of falling asleep with Mark in our double bed, then, when I woke, as I invariably did, an hour or two later, with the bedside light still on and the radio giving me some report about the coffee harvest in Burundi, I would move to the dark and quiet of the spare-room bed and spend the rest of the night there. Mark felt this nocturnal abandonment as a personal rejection, and believed I was exaggerating the impact of his 'love purring', as he liked to call it. After he died, I read in a psychiatric report, dating to one of his hospital stays, that he had cited my preference for a separate bedroom as evidence of the bad state of our relationship. Perhaps it was. However, when we moved into the house in Grantham, I was determined that I should have a quiet, dark bed of my own to retreat to. A few months after the move, Mark was issued with a hospital bed and an air mattress to prevent him getting bed sores from the bed that had become his prison, and the wheezing of the air pump added to the cacophony of his room. I would have found it irksome, but Mark did not mind the noise. He had his treasured radio next to the bed, together with his laptop, on which he worked while he could, checked the news and answered emails. From Argos, I bought an overbed table, which functioned as a dining tray for him as well as a work desk.

Since Mark had been obliged to surrender his driving licence and had then lost his sense of taste and smell, I had gradually taken over the shopping and cooking, on top of the laundry, housework and family admin which I had always done anyway. Also, my demented mother was calling up to a dozen times a day from her new care home, and I was trying to sort out the house and deal with new high-pressure developments at work, so I think, in those first few weeks in Grantham, I neglected Mark a bit. Although I took care of him in a practical sense, helping him with washing and dressing, managing his catheter, making his food, I did not spend much time just sitting with him, keeping him company, chatting about the news. Mark became another category of chore, something that needed organizing, maintaining, ticking off the daily list. There was so much to be done, so much life- and home- and child-organizing, and fitting it in around my new, long commute to Leicester for the job I was still supposed to be doing full-time occupied my whole mind. I was a tornado – very active, but maybe not very effective – picking up telephones, children, shopping, work deadlines, family finances, and whirling them around, clearing a path through our lives by flinging things willy-nilly in all directions. I was convinced that, if I could only get through the to-do list, I would be OK. We would be on top of things. We would be prepared. I forgot that talking and listening had always been the glue in our relationship. I let preparation for life get in the way of actual life. I forgot, in my scuttle of jobs and arrangements, that I loved him. My memory of that time is that I was doing everything, and Mark was unable to help, but I know I must be mistaken. Research on the division of chores within the household shows that both partners significantly overestimate their own contribution and underestimate their partner's. There are whole areas of household activity which are regularly untaken by one person, and their partner never even notices. Men are worse offenders than women, but we are all liable to overestimate the time we spend on jobs and the share of work we do, and we all fail to acknowledge what the other person is doing. Researchers call it egocentric bias. It was egocentric bias that allowed Mark to assume I would have plenty of time to cut his hair a few years earlier, and egocentric bias which made me think I was already, when he presented me with the clippers, doing the lion's share of the housework and life admin. At the time of his illness, our situation was undeniably different from most households, because Mark did not have the physical capacity to do much housework. But, in the New Year, when he spent several weeks in hospital, two things happened that showed me I was guilty of making the same mistaken assumptions. First, our sharp kitchen knives went blunt; and, second, all the houseplants dried up and died.

My days that December were full. While Adam had already started school in Grantham, Greg was not starting his new school till January, so I had to drive him half an hour to Melton each morning and then collect him each afternoon at the end of after-school club. In between, I tried to cram what should have been a full-time professional job, but I seemed to be missing deadlines and letting down colleagues and students all the time, and I didn't have the spare energy to address or even feel guilty about my inadequacy as a scholar and teacher. Then I had to fit in shopping, cooking, dinner, laundry, and I passed what was left of the evenings unpacking boxes and trying to make the house nice, writing Christmas cards and wrapping presents. Mark was finding it harder to get around. He could still manage most of his own personal care, and was able to go downstairs in the morning and back up at the end of the day. However, he could no longer stand for more than a few seconds, or walk more than a few steps. A high stool in the kitchen helped him to sit at the counter and make toast or tea, but I know he was frustrated that he could not do more to help. He used to sit and watch me scurry about, and his helplessness only added to his depression. He rarely got to see other adults, and I was not a relaxing presence. That year, Greg took to singing a little Christmas carol to himself that went, 'Silent night, holy night. All is calm. Except Mum.'

Christmas, apart from Christmas dinner, was always my responsibility anyway, and usually I tried to do it properly: nice presents, home-made cakes and decorations. We used to make paper chains, the children competing to string together the longest one, and then loop them up and down the hall. I would spend the weeks beforehand making candied orange and Christmas-pudding flavour ice cream. Mark was in charge of ordering the turkey and cooking our dinner, which was always excellent. We bought our turkeys from Botterill's farm, in Croxton Kerrial, about ten miles out of Melton. There was always a crowd of people picking up their birds on Christmas Eve, and the farmer's family set up a distribution system from one of their outbuildings. Whenever I go to collect the bird, as I still do, I remember our neighbour, Mark Coleman. The last time I saw him was at Botterill's, when we were both collecting poultry for our family Christmases. He had seemed well and cheerful as we exchanged jokes about goose fat. I did not know that he had terminal cancer. In fact, just over a week later, he died – at home, in bed, while fireworks welcomed 2011. The end of Mark Coleman's life came far too soon, but his death sounds like a good one – at home, with his family around him. He knew what was coming and was able to spend some precious time with his children, and there was time for the family to say the things they needed to say. My Mark spent far longer in bed and died alone. His was not a good death. Mark Coleman's widow, Gail, has been source of inspiration, supporting their three children on her own since her husband's death, and then finding happiness again with a man she met at the flying club when she was getting her pilot's licence. Altogether the coolest of widows.

In 2015, I had not managed to order anything from Botterill's in time. Instead, I made a late dash to Asda and bought a tired-looking, shrink-wrapped, oven-ready turkey, and a last-minute tree, which spewed needles across the car, the drive and all over the carpets as I brought it into the house. I draped some tinsel over the emaciated tree and tied a bunch of balloons to the curtain rail, and that was all we had by way of festive decoration, as I had not got round to buying the materials for paper chains or doing crafty things with sticks and glitter for the windows. Presents were bought in a single Amazon binge, and topped off with some tat I grabbed from the discount shops in town. To my surprise, the lack of home-made candied orange, free-range turkey, locally grown tree and handcrafted decorations mattered not a whit to the children. Something to unwrap on Christmas morning, a lunch involving roast potatoes, and an afternoon in front of a film, eating enough chocolate to put them into a coma, was a perfectly satisfactory outcome.

But I was too stressed to enjoy Christmas Day. Everyone got their presents and their Christmas dinner, and once I had stacked the dishwasher and collected the bits of Christmas cracker from under the table, I locked myself in the bathroom and sobbed. Our usual habit in previous years had been to go for a walk on Christmas afternoon, in what was left of the light, but that year the children could not be prised from their presents and selection boxes, and Mark was too weak and cold to be able to leave the house, so I found myself wandering alone around our new, unfamiliar neighbourhood. It was not cold enough for snow, but the wind was chilly and the sky the pale grey of old knickers. I walked past some allotments beside the railway line and ended up on an open wound of a building site, formerly the edge of a farm, but now the location of a huge, new housing development. Pallets of bricks and tiles loomed in the twilight, plastic sheeting snapping and rattling in the wind. Cold clay oozed on the muddy ground, and fingers of water sneaked inside my shoes. I was cold, lonely, anxious, without any plan and feeling hopeless, vowing that I would never have another Christmas like this one again. As it happens, I never did.

10

THE 6,000-YEAR-OLD QUADRIPLEGIC

There is a problem with the notion that the survival of an individual with a physical impairment is evidence of a compassionate society. In a nutshell, it is that 'disability' is a cultural understanding, and what counts as a disability in one context would not necessarily be recognized as such in another. Therefore, the fact that 'disabled' people apparently lived long lives and had normal burials does not have to mean that economically or socially 'useless' individuals were charitably supported and tolerated only because of the kindness of other people's hearts; it could equally, or more probably, mean that they possessed abilities – practical, intellectual, spiritual or whatever – which were of value to their group, or that their disabilities were simply not relevant. In societies which would have contained people of a range of different ages and states of physical and mental health – including pregnant and post-parturient women, temporarily injured and diseased people – having dwarfism or a spinal deformation would not necessarily have represented a particular impediment to most activities. Indeed, even within a specific diagnosis, individuals vary in what help they need. There is in fact nothing in the condition of the Romito 2 dwarf which would have made him unable to participate in most subsistence activities. Although he might have found walking tiring due to his stature, there is no reason why he should have been unable to travel with the rest of the group without particular assistance. After all, children, who are also short, would not necessarily expect to be carried after the age of four or five. People manage. Whatever people might have preferred to think, Richard III managed to rule a country, plot against his enemies and lead his army into battle, despite having a spinal deformity.

Sometimes, though, the physical condition of an individual's remains leaves us in little doubt that, by any standard, they were seriously disabled. Consider Man Bac, burial 9. M9, as this individual is known, died somewhere between 3,700 and 4,000 years ago, at the site of Man Bac, in northern Vietnam. He was a young man of about twenty-five. Looking at the photographs taken during excavation, it is immediately obvious, even to a non-specialist, that something is not right. He is lying on his side, with his knees and elbows flexed. The long bones of his arms and legs, which should be as thick as a good-sized carrot, are as thin as pencils. His burial position is not typical of others in the cemetery, possibly due to difficulties positioning his body, but he was buried carefully and accompanied by a round, cord-impressed terracotta pot. Further analysis of his bones revealed a lengthy inventory of abnormalities. Not only were his bones exceptionally thin, the joints of his jaw were degraded and parts of his spine had fused solid. He would have had no movement in his lower body, and none, or very little, in his upper body either. Based on modern clinical knowledge, the osteo-archaeologists who analysed his remains thought that he probably had Klippel–Feil Syndrome, a rare genetic disorder in which the vertebrae of the neck become fused. Numerous other abnormalities can affect people with this condition, including problems with their circulatory, respiratory, nervous and intestinal systems, among others. M9's paralysis probably came on around the age of fifteen, so, for at least a decade, from the onset of symptoms to his death, he would have needed extensive support and care from others to stay alive.

M9's helplessness and vulnerability placed heavy demands on those caring for him. He would have been unable to acquire food or water for himself and, because of the restricted movement of his head, neck and jaw, would prob-ably also have needed help to eat and drink. He would have needed to be clothed against the cool, damp winters, and positioned on a soft surface, off the wet ground. Whoever was looking out for him would have needed to ensure that dangers were kept at bay, since he could not move himself away from sun, insects, animals or other everyday hazards. Unable to move much, if at all, he would have needed to be carried to any new location, and, because his bones were so light and thin, moving him would have had to be done carefully, so that his fragile arms and legs did not break. The risk of pressure sores developing and becoming infected is very high. Even in modern clinical settings, they can be hard to avoid. Mark had the beginnings of one, despite regular washing, repositioning and an automatic air mattress.

Infection takes hold quickly in dirty or wet skin, so M9 would have needed regular washing, toileting and help to keep his skin clean and dry. His body would have needed to be moved and maybe massaged frequently to avoid sores. The absence of any evidence of infection in the bone shows that M9's carers managed to prevent severe pressure sores. Similarly, the absence of evidence of fractures on his remains testify to the delicacy with which he was carried, repositioned and massaged.

M9's survival for about ten years from the onset of his paralysis was only possible if he received constant and skilled care. We cannot know whether he had a single carer or many, or whether his carers were family or not, but we can say that, since the care he needed was so extensive and time-consuming, it would have seriously reduced the time and energy his carers were able to give to the basic work of feeding and caring for themselves and their families. It seems likely, then, that the whole community supported M9 and recognized the value of caring for him, even when they must have realized that he was not likely to get better, and that he was unable to contribute materially to the well-being of the community, whatever his contribution in other ways might have been.

The case of M9, and a few others like him, raise questions for archaeologists interested in the origins and development of compassion. Those who demand a Darwinian explanation for all observed human behaviour want to know why, from an evolutionary perspective, this kind of long-term care-giving even happened. It subjects the care-giver to additional stress and offers no clear benefit to either the individual carer or their community. The answer, for everyone else, is that not every behaviour has to be adaptive, that respect for life and tenderness towards people who are suffering are part of what gives life its shape and meaning.

So, what does the burial of M9 mean? It means, says Lorna Tilley, who studied his bones, that he was an emotionally resilient man with a strong will to live. Given the high rate of psychological problems among paraplegics and quadriplegics, we can infer that he was socially engaged with a community that supported him, that he was positive and optimistic. But I am also struck by what we might say about another person or people in Man Bac: M9's carer. Here was somebody without shops, showers, piped water, soap or information about a rare disease; without wheelchairs or disabled living aids. And this somebody, living in a time and place without even houses, draught animals or, possibly, agriculture, given that all the food evidence from the site suggests that they were hunter-gatherers, had the physical, emotional, economic and social resources to care for a profoundly impaired young man for a decade. It puts me to shame.

What was she like, this carer from 4,000 years ago? I am imagining a woman, though it might not have been. Was she his mother? Was she looking after other children too, a baby at the breast or on her hip as she held a cup to his lips? Did he have siblings or cousins playing round him while she positioned him on his chamber pot or washed and dried his skin on a sweaty summer day? Did she have friends, relatives and neighbours who gave some of their time to prepare meals for them, of fish, fruit and nuts? I hope so. I hope she felt tender and not angry. I hope she had help.

Whereas he had been able, in December, to come downstairs in the morning and spend the day in the kitchen and living room, secretly sharpening knives and watering the plants, by January 2016, Mark was struggling to make those daily trips up and down the stairs, and sometimes he did not come down at all.

On the morning of 15 January, Mark and I managed the awkward waltz from bed to bathroom and into the shower. He had a fold-down stool in the shower cubicle, and found the sensation of warm water on his skin a relief from the crawling, itching sensation that plagued his back. Afterwards, we got him dry and dressed, and staggered him back to bed. The whole process left him weak and exhausted. Once he was back in bed and resting, I went downstairs to make us some tea. I had only been in the kitchen a couple of minutes when, over the noise of the kettle, I heard Mark calling me in a voice of panic. When I got upstairs to him, he told me that his legs were completely paralysed – so unresponsive that he could not even twitch them. His speech was starting to slur. He was terrified. As I sat with him, hoping that this would pass, his arms and hands also became weaker and weaker, until they too were totally immobile. His pulse was still strong and his breathing normal, but I was worried that he was having a stroke. I called an ambulance. While we waited for it to arrive, he lost the ability to move even his face. His eyes were closed and he could not open them. He could barely move his lips. At that time, he told me later, he was pretty sure he was dying, that this was his body shutting down. He was trying to tell me something, but his voice was so quiet and slurred, it was hard to make out. Then I understood he was trying to list his various computer and banking passwords. Five hundred years ago, a person facing imminent death would pray for absolution; a hundred years ago, maybe they'd pass on a life lesson to their children; in our secular age, our last words are more likely to comprise a random assortment of at least eight characters, including upper- and lower- case letters, and a minimum of one number and one special character such as !*?£.

'Yes, don't worry. I've got that,' I said, though I had not retained any of his passwords, nor was I prepared to devote even the smallest part of my mind at that moment to memorizing log-ins.

The ambulance took forever to get to us, and there was not much I could do, except sit on Mark's bed, occasionally wiping his face with a flannel – not because he was dirty, but because it was a sensation he could feel, and I hoped it would let him know he was not alone, and he might not be so scared. This was only the second time I had ever ridden in an ambulance. A few years earlier, I had gone to A and E with Greg after a fall had left him slightly concussed. It was interesting to be on the other side of those one-way windows, but the comfortless interior and the sideways sitting made me feel a bit sick. When I was a child, the ambulances racing past with their mysterious windows had always seemed a bit glamourous and exciting. I wanted the chance to go in one, like I wanted to ride in a helicopter. The reality was less fun: not so much like a luxury caravan as a work minivan, all boxes of equipment and bare metal sides. I have heard that helicopters are similarly disappointing inside.

In the end, the Queen's Medical Centre in Nottingham kept him in over the weekend and arranged an ambulance transfer to take him from there directly to the John Radcliffe in Oxford. This was originally planned as a short stay, so that his consultant could run another bunch of tests, but it ended up lasting many weeks.

Back at home, I went to the doctor on my own account, hoping for some sleeping tablets or some pharmaceutical solution to my stress and insomnia, but, when I started crying in his office, he signed me off work for a month instead.

I saw few people at that time, apart from the children. While I was on leave from the university, I worked on the house, cleaning up the hall floor and turning the pre-kitchen into a downstairs bedroom for Mark. I did my best to patch up the plaster in there, painted the walls yellow, his favourite colour, and bought a day bed from Ikea, which I put together over a couple of evenings. I put up some pictures and bought new lampshades, pale yellow bed linen and a cream carpet. This was before I found out what can happen after a fall between the bed and the commode. I hoped he would be happy to be downstairs, close to family life, although, when he eventually came home, he decided he would prefer to be in his own bed upstairs, and he never even sat on the daybed or dozed in the yellow room.

I was quite proud of myself for decorating Mark's new

bedroom, and for fitting new taps in the downstairs loo, but, in truth, I felt desperately out of my depth trying to do DIY jobs on my own. I am definitely more of a cerebral than a practical type, and, like many women, I had come – rather feebly, I know – to rely on the man in the house for anything involving power tools, plumbing or heavy work. It was liberating and a little embarrassing to find out how easy it was to use the hedge-trimmer or the electric drill. One night, however, as I was drawing the curtains in the lounge, the whole curtain rail came away from the wall. Our lounge had very tall, old and heavy sliding doors along the back wall, and it was the rail above these that had come away. I knew I would have to level and fasten a new rail, which meant using the drill and trying, on my own, to hold a long rail in position while I fixed it, balanced on the ladder. I wanted to cry. I phoned my sister-in-law and expressed my trepidation.

'I don't know how to do it properly. Perhaps I'll just get a man in.'

'Yes,' she said, sympathizing. 'Take your mind off the whole curtain-rail situation.'

But, the following weekend, my sister-in-law, my brother and their four children gamely rolled up, clutching an electric drill and a spirit level, to help with the curtain rail, and to finish painting the shelves in the front room. What good eggs.

Jon, my brother-in-law, called me in late January.

'I've been thinking about your situation, about the house.'

'Oh, yes?'

'Mmmm. And I think there is a danger that you could come to hate the house, because it is just a list of jobs to do by yourself and a source of stress. So, I have two suggestions. First, get a decorator in to do some of the work. You can afford it and it will be a weight off. And, second, I think you should choose one room to be a refuge, and get that room done first. Then, you'll have at least one place where you can relax.'

I decided to take both pieces of advice. The hall, stairs and landing were high spaces, the ceilings precarious to reach. A professional would be quicker and safer. Because it was Jon's suggestion, not mine, that meant I wasn't being lazy. I had permission to get help. And, in the meantime, I started work on my bedroom. I took up the carpets and arranged for somebody to come to sand and polish the floorboards. I painted the walls the richest blue I could find. On my way home from Leicester one day, I found myself stuck in traffic outside a furniture showroom on Frog Island. The chunky, solid designs appealed to me, so, while Mark was in hospital, I took the three children, plus Rachel's boyfriend, on a shopping trip and rashly ordered a new bed – high and heavy, with huge square posts and solid head and foot boards. In a magazine in the doctor's waiting room, I saw a picture of a light fitting that looked like a big brass lotus flower. I ordered one of those, too. Bright new bed linen – blue, to match the walls – was quite easy to find. My room, my choices, which I did not need to justify to anyone else, so I got decent, high thread-count sheets, which Mark would have called a waste of money, but they felt cool and smooth to me, a source of tactile pleasure. I found a snapshot of the three kids from the day Greg was born: Rachel, aged eight, looks seriously at the camera; Adam is grinning and slightly blurry as he tries to get down from the sofa; and laid across both of their laps is brand-new Gregory in a turquoise Babygro. I put it in a cheap frame next to my bed, on top of the wooden chest full of Christmas decorations, which I was using as a bedside table. A lamp, my diary, a couple of novels and this picture. The bedroom felt like mine. It smelt of floorboards and paint and hand cream. Through the window, I could see mostly trees, but, in winter, when the leaves have dropped, there is a view of the railway line. I got to know the different train sounds – the InterCity, the slow chugger to Nottingham, the clattering freight trains in the middle of the night – and the three-note alarm of the track warning siren, and the alternating notes heralding the approach of a fast train whooshing through the town.

I did not mention it to anyone at the time, because people expected me to be eager to bring Mark home and to be worried about him being in hospital, but it was an emancipation having him staying somewhere else. I knew he was safe and cared for, but there was nothing I had to do, and nobody looking over my shoulder or complaining about the children or the world in general. There was a lightness in the house. The children were also in holiday mood. We were all getting on well, dancing in the kitchen, watching telly together, having their friends round. On Adam's birthday that year, with Mark still in the hospital in Oxford, the two boys and I went up to meet Rachel at her university. By Adam's choice, we had a largely vegetable-free dinner of burgers and sweet-potato fries in a chain restaurant that Mark would not have approved of.

Although the separation was a welcome relief for me, a chance to regroup, to get some more sleep, to begin getting the house organized, Mark was finding the prolonged hospital stay boring and lonely. The stroke, or whatever it was, had been followed by another similar episode in hospital that same night, and then by three more episodes over the next couple of weeks, while he was at Oxford. The first time it happened, he had been unable to move even his mouth or his eyelids. Through all of them, he was half expecting that he would not be able to breathe, or that his tongue would slide into his throat, or that in some other way he would lose consciousness and die. At those moments, or as soon as possible afterwards, he wanted to talk to me; he wanted reassurance, familiarity, family, and I was the only person who could give him that. He was Moriens without the deathbed consolers, a modern everyman facing death alone and scared. In his better hours, he enjoyed observing hospital life. He had a view over the suburbs and, in the foreground, to his great delight, the hospital helipad, so he could watch the air ambulance come and go. I had assumed, as he had, that the air ambulance was mostly used for transporting critically ill patients to the hospital when their condition was super urgent – people cut out of cars after traffic accidents, or who were deteriorating so rapidly, they could not risk a delay on the roads. But the nurse told Mark that mostly the helicopter was taking and collecting transplant organs. He was happy to think that the sound of the blades whumping through the air was somebody being saved, rather than somebody probably dying.

So, there was an asymmetry between us: Mark, bored and lonely and wanting to be at home; me, soaking up the relative calm and freedom of a temporary respite from care duties and from our fractious relationship. In the end, due to the other events, to recurrent infections and attempts at new treatments, Mark stayed in Oxford for five weeks, and then was discharged to our local hospital in Grantham, where he was to continue with antibiotic treatment for an ongoing infection. This was much easier for us: I could visit every day, bringing new books, newspapers and clean clothes. The children could see their father again. Even this increased level of contact, however, was far short of the normal home life that Mark longed for. He continued to press the hospital staff to speed up his discharge, assuring them, I found out later, that he would have plenty of support at home and that his house was well adapted to his needs and abilities. None of the medical staff at the hospital ever asked me about that. On Monday, 7 March, he was discharged from Grantham back to our house. He was delighted to be home. I was not delighted to have him there.

11

FIELD SCHOOL

Soon after starting at Leicester, a colleague and I launched a new postgraduate degree in historical archaeology. It was mainly designed to be studied by distance learning, but we decided that one element of the course should bring our students from around the world together, in Leicester, for a week. We devised a full programme of field trips, lectures and activities. The students were highly motivated and – having taken a week away from their jobs, families and other responsibilities to pursue a passion – exuberant and energetic. It was intense and exhausting to teach, but became my favourite work week of the year. In the early days, my chief collaborator on the field-school module was my head of department, Marilyn Palmer. A senior and influential industrial archaeologist, Marilyn had boundless enthusiasm and an impish sense of fun which made her popular with students. At that time, she was working on a project for the National Trust, on country house technology. When urban areas upgraded to gas or electric light, piped water and sewerage, and the plethora of labour-saving devices afforded by new technologies of power in the eighteenth and nineteenth centuries, she explained, Britain's stately homes, in their isolated and often remote locations, were rarely part of the transformation. Because they needed their own gas plants, generators or hydraulic engineering, the timing and nature of their adoption of novel schemes depended on other factors. One of these was the character of the owner. Some were enthusiastic followers of innovation in science and engineering, who proved to be early adopters. Others were traditionalists who resisted change. Calke Abbey, in Derbyshire, one of our first field-school destinations, did not get electric lighting until 1962. What struck me most about Marilyn's research, though, was the complementary relationship she noticed between technology and human labour. When servants were cheap and plentiful, the benefits of technology, for the people who paid for it, were marginal. They never had to empty their own closed stools or clean their own grates anyway, and, if they wanted a hot bath, they only needed to instruct somebody else to fill the tub with hot water. The landowning classes rarely thought about the discomfort involved in making them comfortable. A household with piped hot water and flushing toilets, on the other hand, could manage with fewer servants and therefore less expense. No army of helpers was required to run up and down stairs all day with buckets of hot water or chamber pots. Even after Marilyn retired, I liked to pass on to the students her observations about how the adoption of technological solutions varied with labour costs. Technology substitutes for people.

It is not just a historical issue. The way that new technologies can do the work that was formerly done by people

– especially low-paid people, doing dull or repetitive work – is a theme of our contemporary conversations. It is a good thing, I am sure, when drudgery can be reduced. However, technology is not always a solution, and there are dark sides. Livelihoods can be lost. Sometimes, technology has an ideological role in shutting down people's real concerns. For example, we have washing machines and dishwashers and vacuum cleaners now, so housework is no longer a full-time job to be done by a housewife or a maid. It is emancipating and it means that women can go out to work. However, it does not eliminate the need for housework to be done entirely, and there is a risk that the existence of those friendly robots makes it harder for people – usually women, for cultural reasons – to ask for extra help, or companionship, reassurance and human time.

At six o'clock on the morning of 7 March 2016, I got up to make a cup of tea and bring it back to bed, steeling myself for the day ahead. Mark was due home from hospital that day and I was nauseous with dread. He was not cured, but by this point the doctors had run out of things to do to him. We would now have to wait and see what the result of the last round of treatments had been. He could not really walk – could barely move at all, in fact – and there was no prospect that this was going to change. An ambulance brought him home and, with help from the ambulance driver, I moved him into the kitchen and made him some coffee. Now what? I did not know how to look after this man or even how to relate to him. Although he did not have dementia, his brain damage was certainly changing the way he behaved and spoke. The psychiatrist said he was a 'textbook' subcortical case. According to Wikipedia, this meant, in behavioural terms, that he might be less able to identify or empathize with the emotions of others, his behaviour might be uninhibited and his thought processes sometimes strange or hard to follow. These were all true for Mark. He was still clever, and his previously excellent memory was mostly good, except for some odd lapses – like when he forgot our youngest child's name or could not remember which town we lived in. He was not demented, but he was often hard to follow. He was bad-tempered with the children and upset them by accusing them of things they had not done or ascribing bad motives to the things they had done. I did not know how much of that was due to his brain damage, and how much was simply the understandable result of his circumstances making him mardy and exacerbating a natural tendency towards misanthropy.

It all felt very different from my father's final illness, seven years earlier. Dad was diagnosed with mesothelioma, an incurable cancer of the lining of the lung. It is almost always associated with exposure to asbestos, often decades before the cancer is detectable. Dad's was probably related to a job he did in his twenties, which involved walking through tunnels alongside pipes that were lagged with asbestos. At a time before I was even born, he inhaled a tiny particle that caused his death forty-five years later. He had chemotherapy, which extended his life by maybe six or nine months, but died about a year after diagnosis. The quality of Dad's last year, however, was quite different from Mark's. He went on holiday to Florida, and my parents rode bikes and went on walks. He patched up an argument with his brother that dated back more than forty years, to the time when he had decided to marry my mother, a Methodist, and was cut off by his Jewish family. All his children and grandchildren spent time with him. I have a photo of us all together that final New Year, four months before he died, Dad grinning broadly from under his woolly hat, while the kids played in the country park. He put his affairs in order, as the saying goes, but also had time to reassure us that he was happy with his life, that he did not have a sense of adventures unhad or ambitions unfulfilled. He lived and died a happy man. He was at home until only hours before his death, cared for by my mother and visited by Macmillan nurses. The last time I saw him was about a week before his death. He could not walk far then, but was sufficiently mobile to ride in the car with my mother and me to a lake near their house and stand on the shore. We ate cashew nuts and talked about inconsequential things. I still miss him.

On the day Mark came home, he had dinner downstairs with the family for the first time in nearly two months. He was in a good mood that evening, happy to be back home with us. I knew it was better for his mental health, and I tried to focus on that and not on how it would feel in the house, but I had tasted the open air. Returning to the oppressive sense that I was being watched and judged, that I needed to be vigilant at all times to protect the children's feelings, was suffocating. There seemed no future in which our relationship could be made easy. The following morning, I woke up at 4 a.m. and just cried. I had never felt so hopeless, so trapped, so utterly miserable. I was marinating in self-pity, which was only displaced when I went into Mark's room at waking-up time to bring him a cup of tea, and found his bed, duvet, everything soaked in urine after a catheter accident.

I changed the bed, and Mark. He was exhausted after the changing, and probably also from the transfer home the previous day, so he slept most of the day, until the evening, when he had another accident and soiled the bed. I helped him up and he managed to get, very slowly, and with help, to the bathroom for a shower, but afterwards he collapsed on the step outside the bathroom door, and could not get back up. I could not lift him enough for him to use either the wheelchair or the walking frame. Eventually we found that, if he lay on his back and I lifted his knees and placed his feet flat on the floor, he could shuffle backwards on his elbows a few inches. Then he fell, utterly worn out, into bed and slept for the rest of the night.

That first week was a round of physios, occupational therapists, GPs, deliveries of equipment and supplies, phone calls and so on, as I tried to arrange for some carers to come in and help with breakfast, lunch and washing, so that I could go to work. Even so, the situation did not seem sustainable. Friends told me that it was important for me to continue with my job, for psychological reasons and to maintain a life outside the home, but it was getting increasingly hard.

Our field-school week usually fell in April. I was nervous,

that year, about leaving Mark and being unable to get to him
if he needed urgent help. I arranged for my colleague to
drive the students out from Leicester, so I could come in my
own car and would be able to get home quickly if I had to.
I met the students by the church in the village of Kirby
Bellars, to escort them down the footpath to a couple of
fields full of interesting traces of medieval Leicestershire. The
first time I came here, it was because Mark and I had spotted
a long, linear feature from the train on our way from Melton
to Leicester and had decided to investigate. There turned
out to be real archaeological riches in those fields: a deserted
medieval village, a series of fish ponds, some ornamental
garden features and a large moated site, as well as numerous
quarries and the visible traces of several old roads. I used to
ask the students to describe what they could see and then
discuss what might have produced those patterns. It was an
exercise in looking deeply and making connections, in skill
rather than knowledge. In the afternoon, we would do something similar in another nearby village, only examining
standing buildings instead of landscape features, trying to
describe what we saw and reconstruct the sequence of events
that made a house or a church look the way it does. It is the
kind of fieldwork I like best: learning from each other,
working as a team to develop our story. For the students –
who had, at this point in their studies, spent a year working
alone, using the texts and handbooks we supplied by post
– it was a chance to ask questions, to chat with each other,
to feel part of a community. Posting videos online and
sending round a carefully prepared FAQs document could

not supply the richness of educational experience and human understanding that we all got from walking together over those green spring meadows, littered with the docked tails of that season's lambs, trying to follow the line of a ditch with our eyes and hands and feet. It was a clear illustration to me of how technology could not adequately and entirely replace people.

I managed only one day of the field school, that year. On all the others, Mark was too ill to be left at home for more than a few hours. As on many occasions in those months, I found myself unable to engage with my work; sometimes, when I did drive to my office in Leicester, I would then receive a call from Mark to say that he had fallen or had an accident that needed cleaning up, so I would have to turn around and go straight back home, anyway. I was feeling guilty about how little I had seen my colleagues and aware of how much extra work they must have been silently shouldering to compensate for my absence or general uselessness. I arranged formally to reduce my working hours.

The days went on, slowly and hopelessly. Mark's pain came and went, but increasingly it came and stayed. His skin burned. His feet spasmed uncontrollably. His eyesight would fail often, for several hours at a time, so all he could do was lie in his bed, listening to the radio. In the first few weeks at home, he tried, on his better days, to come downstairs – going to the top of the staircase either on his bum or using the frame or wheelchair, then shuffling down the stairs by sitting on each step and easing himself down to the next one. At the bottom, I would help turn him round and get him into the wheelchair, so he could go into the kitchen. The procedure was repeated in reverse in the evening. But, on many days, he did not have the energy to change rooms, or even to get out of bed. The itchy skin on his back and legs was a constant source of irritation, and, because it was neurological, no treatment of the skin could give him any lasting relief; all he had was the temporary comfort of me rubbing his back with moisturizer. During this period, his skin was probably softer than it had ever been in his life.

After a couple of weeks of waiting to hear from social services about arranging carers for Mark, I found out that, whether they were organized by adult social care or privately, we would still have to pay the whole cost ourselves, so I spent an hour ringing round and found a local company who promised to send out somebody later that day to meet us and discuss what we needed. Two women arrived in the early afternoon and, after chatting with us both, we ended up with an agreement that they would start coming twice a day, mornings and lunchtimes, from the following Monday. It would make it possible for me to go into Leicester for work, and take off some of the practical burden. Then, two hours later, one of them phoned up and told me that, on reflection, they had decided they could not help with Mark's care after all. They were used to looking after much older men, they told me, and would feel uncomfortable providing intimate care to a man of Mark's age.

'They don't trust themselves around an Adonis like me,' said Mark, wryly.

I was furious, but there was nothing I could do except get

back to ringing care providers, and I eventually found another firm who agreed to take on Mark. The carers would help get his breakfast and lunch, help him use the commode, empty his catheter bag, if necessary, and help him wash his hands and face and clean his teeth in the morning.

The days went on. I was getting so little work done now, and feeling stressed and tearful all the time – not just caring for Mark, but trying to sort out the horrible house that needed so much doing to it, and was cold and smelled of damp. And my mother, whose dementia was worsening at this time, was calling many times a day, often in distress, wanting to go 'home', wondering where my long-dead father was. She had taken to phoning up at odd hours of the night, sometimes several times in a single night, to ask questions or simply to have a chat. Often, she wanted to let me know she was away from home 'in this place', and wanted me to let my sister and brother know. She had no idea that it was 4.30 in the morning, or that 4.30 in the morning was not a normal time to call your daughter, or that she had already called me, and my brother and sister, earlier that night. The uncertainty of the future, of how long this might go on for, made me angry, and, in my anger, frustration and exhaustion, I was snappy with the boys and very short-tempered with Mark. I said hurtful things to him and then berated myself for being so unkind. Knowing that my anger came from extreme fatigue, uncertainty and powerlessness did not make it go away. I realized that, bad as I felt, it was ten times worse for Mark. He was more powerless, more frustrated, and also in pain and misery, facing the prospect that he would never recover.

Looking back on it, I was probably quite close to the far limits of what I was able to cope with. I noticed with surprise, in a kind of disembodied way, how far things could go without me actually having a breakdown.

I hardly knew who I was any more. I was self-pitying, boring, angry. I was bone-weary. I did not know what would happen. I was impatient. I did not want to sit quietly until things worked themselves out; I went looking, instead. I made so many plans. I even bought a notebook – black, businessy, hardbacked and severely ruled – on the first page of which I wrote *PLANS* and underlined it twice. The rest of the book reads like a PhD in formal logic: *IF M.'s results have come through and show evidence of cancer, THEN he could start treatment by the end of this month, and IF that works, he could be walking again by Christmas.* I had become an unrewarding conversationalist. People asked me constantly about how Mark was, but I could not give any clear answers. There were no real facts. Inevitably, I could not say what our friends wanted to hear: We know what it is, now; this is what it means; this is what will happen; this is what will become of him, of me, of us. Right until the end, all his treatments, his symptoms, his hospital visits, his changing capacities were plotless. There was no clear narrative to Mark's illness. I called it progressive, but the direction of travel was uncertain. I could not produce the kind of tale that our friends and relatives wanted to be told – too much was unknown, there were too few fixed points. We did not know what kind of a story we were in.

Our last visit to Oxford was on Friday, 1 April. I was up

by five o'clock, so I could get Mark dressed and downstairs into the car. We left the house at about 6.30. In the end, we had more than three hours with Dr Leite and with Mary Quirke, the specialist neurology nurse. They took lots of notes, examined Mark, took more samples. But the result of everything was that the disease still had no known cause, his illness was getting worse and worse. Even the achingly optimistic Dr Leite had, for the first time, used the word 'progressive'. She had always held out the hope that a way would be found for Mark to get better, but now, finally, she was willing to say that the aim of treatment was no longer to reverse or cure the disease, but to slow its progress. Mark's great fear, and mine too, was that, if Dr Leite succeeded in slowing or stalling the steady advance of the disease, he would be facing maybe twenty years of the same thing, or of slow, slow deterioration, just accumulating time, just getting more of it. That did not sound like a desirable goal.

Mark seemed to be taking this news quite well. I was not sure whether this was because he had not really understood what we were being told, or whether he was just buoyed up by seeing Dr Leite and moved by having so much of her time and attention.

While I craved knowledge about Mark's condition, even if it meant embracing a bad prognosis, Mark did not want to know bad news. He was of a naturally more optimistic temperament than me anyway, and I can see why, for him, there was comfort in being able to think that he would recover. For as long as he had no diagnosis and no prognosis, he could pretend that his illness was temporary, and we could go on planning for a future in which he would be making salamis and working in the garden, watching the kids grow up and eventually supporting me so that I could take financial and career risks too.

I wanted to know one way or the other: would he live or die? If we had been told that Mark's condition had stabilized and that we should expect him to stay as he was, we would have made better decisions about how to adapt the house – or, indeed, about moving to such an unsuitable house in the first place. Mary, the specialist nurse, had endless suggestions for devices and changes that we could make to the house to facilitate looking after Mark: fitting a stairlift; putting ramps up the external steps and over internal changes in floor level. When he first came home from hospital, Mark had wanted to be upstairs in his own bed. He had a walking frame and a wheelchair, neither of which could be used on the stairs. Before his stay in hospital, he had used the chair when he was downstairs and then used the frame to get from the top of the stairs to his bed, and between bedroom and bathroom. But, after his release from hospital in early March, it soon became nearly impossible to make the transfers from sitting on the stairs to sitting in his chair or leaning on the frame. I was not convinced that even a stairlift would be very useful if I could not help him transfer from it to his chair at the top. And there was one question which I dared never voice: is it worth it? I felt guilt for thinking it. Should I not be willing to do anything to make Mark's life even a tiny bit more bearable? Even if it costs thousands of pounds and makes the house into a care home, even if he only uses it for a couple of weeks?

In the hospital, I tried to talk to Mary, the specialist nurse, about the practical problems of taking care of Mark at home. I told her about his falls, about how hard it was to get to the bathroom. I told her about how difficult it was becoming for him to transfer from the bed to the commode, even with my help. I told her about the effort involved in getting him in and out of the house on days when he has hospital appointments, trying to find help to lift him up and down the stairs. For these practical problems, Mary offered practical solutions. She had come prepared to this consultation, pulling from her bag a hefty catalogue, which she now rattled through, stopping to show me something that looked like a big, wide boomerang. A banana board, she told me; Mark and I can use it to move him easily between the bed and the commode or wheelchair. Another page: what appears to be a giant anglepoise lamp on skis. 'A hoist!' Mary beamed. 'That will also help with transfers, or if he has another fall!'

The catalogue is a compendium of clinical-looking equipment, and she urged me to take it home with us. We already had, by then, a walking frame and a wheelchair, an overbed table and a commode. We had grab rails in the shower and by the toilet, from the days when Mark could still use the toilet. We had a hospital bed on order, and cardboard boxes full of spare catheter bags, adult nappies, disposable gloves. We had bed protectors and non-slip floor mats. But we had barely ventured into the grotto of hideousness that is the disability aids catalogue. We could get ramps for the steps outside the back door and to go over the step into the house, and another one to get Mark over the rim of the shower cubicle, though I suspected not for the steep flight of steps up to the front door. We could get leg-lifters, like stirrups on straps, to help Mark move his own, paralysed legs out of the bed. We could get bedside rails to help him ease himself in and out, and a cradle to put over his feet to lift the covers off his lower legs and feet when they burned and crawled with a pain that analgesics were unable to touch. We could have emergency contact alarms and bells, both fitted around the house and mobile, for when I am out.

'Have a look through, and let me know what you want.' Mary seemed pleased to have solved our problems, to have found the things that would help – and they would help, of course. It was my fault for presenting the problems as practical ones, which they were, but it was not the whole story, and none of this helped with the real issue, which was that Mark did not want to be reduced to a lumpen problem of a body, and, whatever the tools available, I did not want to do this job. I found Mary's talk of hoists and boards unutterably depressing. I was not only dismayed by the admission that this was now our life, but also irritated by the breeziness of it. I do not think that Mary was suggesting that, with a few bits of kit, everything would be OK. And, really, what else could she do? But I thought of Marilyn's country houses and the whole issue of meeting human needs with clever devices that ostensibly address the practical problem, but ignore the human operators in their isolation. Our problems were not solved. Why, I wondered, did nobody say, 'This means that your lives as they have been and as you once imagined they would be are effectively over'?

And accepting all the kit that Mary and the occupational therapist tried to give us felt like I was tacitly accepting my new role as a carer – a role which nobody ever discussed with me, or asked if I was prepared to accept; a role which was now, apparently, to be mine before, and maybe to the exclusion of, all others, indefinitely. I wanted to say, petulantly, No, I don't want a hoist and a banana board. I want our lives back. I want to go to work, and I want my worries to be about the departmental reorganization. And, if I can't have my life back, I want you to acknowledge what is happening, and not to pretend that a few bits of equipment will make everything OK, because it is not OK. Nothing about this is OK. It's not OK that Mark is likely to collapse on the floor at any moment, and if I go to work there is a good chance that I will have to come straight home again because Mark has fallen or is in pain and needs me. I am forty-eight and I should be building my career and making plans for the garden, not trooping to the pharmacy every week to collect prescriptions or huge boxes of adult nappies.

I recalled one of Marilyn's country house technology problems, about the introduction of servant bells. I had seen these many times in costume dramas and tours of stately homes: a little row of bells in the kitchen or the butler's pantry, each labelled with a different location in the house. For the owners of the house, they meant that, rather than waiting for a servant to check on them, or going to find one, they could just ring a bell from the bedroom, drawing room or wherever, and a servant would come to see what they needed. An efficiency saving – except, as Marilyn pointed out, if the servant needed was not in the kitchen when the bell rang. If they heard a bell while, for example, cleaning the fireplace in the library, they would have to scurry to the kitchen first to find out which bell was ringing and then go to attend to their employer's need. More efficient for the waited-upon, but another layer of expectation for those doing the waiting. Similarly, I remembered her saying that the acquisition of new technology usually meant a big cut to the number of domestic staff, and that those staff who were left missed the companionship and camaraderie of life below stairs, even though they might benefit from tools which eased the physical burden of their work. This made sense to me. Technology was offered to me as a gift for which I should be grateful, and I was, but it did not obviate the need for community, for human support and understanding.

Through March, April and early May that year, mostly I was just tired. Caring for Mark, managing the house and trying to do enough of my job not to get sacked took up a lot of my life. Emotionally, I was as brittle and dried out as one of the crab shells the kids used to bring home from holiday, wrapped in loo roll and packed into an empty margarine tub. I was too tired to do proper parenting any more. I abandoned the screen-time limit with the boys because I did not have the mental resources to come up with a menu of wholesome alternatives. Now, provided they had done their homework/ music practice/ bedroom tidying, I left them to get on with shooting fireballs at trolls. I thought I might find that cathartic myself.

Some of my well-meaning friends liked to tell me how important it was that, under such stressful circumstances, I take care of myself. I frequently saw similar advice on leaflets and websites for carers. I got sick of hearing the analogy between caring and putting on your own oxygen mask first in a plane, before you help anyone else. There is some truth in this, but really, as advice, it will not do. I found myself resenting it – even sensing when it was about to be hauled out. Oh, not the bloody oxygen-mask thing again. This advice only emphasized the distance between my experience and my friends' ability to comprehend it. Who would look after Mark while I was having my spa break? How would the children be fed and the cupboards kept full? If I gave up work, or did not take on so much, what would we live on? This is one of the silences around the act of caring. It is stressful and super demanding, and stress needs more than the commitment to look after yourself. Society should not be putting an additional responsibility onto carers: their exhaustion is not voluntary. Carers are overwhelmed and burned out, not through some martyrish determination to soldier on unassisted. They are not, for the most part, turning away the legions of friends and relatives who besiege them with home-cooked meals, offers to mow the lawn or stay for the weekend while you take a bit of me-time. Nobody opts into exhaustion if they have a choice. People find themselves, as I did, becoming round-the-clock, round-the-calendar carers because they do not have any alternative. Being told to treat yourself gently is like being told to cheer up or not to worry. Our lives, and this is what makes it so bloody hard, are no longer in our control. Do you not think, I want to ask, that I would breathe the oxygen if it were there? Do you not know that I would suck it like a desperate, guzzling hog?

On Tuesdays, at six o'clock, Adam had guitar lessons from a man called Jan. There was nowhere to park at Jan's house, so, on the dark evenings of our first winter in Grantham, I would drop Adam off, then wait for him in the KFC down the road, reading my library book and drinking nasty, stewed tea out of a corrugated paper cup. As winter turned into spring, however, six o'clock was no longer dark. I swapped the KFC for the car park at the Premier Inn, from where I could walk along the towpath of the Grantham Canal, away from town, and watch the trees develop their hazy green fuzz and, later, see the swans leading their new cygnets through the water, their feathers smirched with thick, green algae. There was not time for a long walk, but these cherished half-hours, and there cannot have been more than half a dozen of them, were islands of positivity. While I savoured the evening light and the quiet minutes alone, though, I knew that Mark's life lacked even those small islands. His was an ocean of pain, tedium and frustration. Most of the time, Mark was stoical about the disease that was taking away his life. He never asked, 'Why me?' or 'Why now?' or complained about the unfairness of it. The closest he came to expressing the arbitrary injustice of it was when I told him about my walk afterwards, and he would often be, reasonably, rueful.

'You're lucky.'

I did not feel lucky, but, looking from his side, I guess I was. I was alive. I could walk, drive, move without pain, make myself a cup of tea when I wanted one. I had no medications to take, no hospital appointments to keep. It was easy for me to spend time with the children, and to look ahead with every expectation that I would watch them grow up, move out, find the roads that would take them through their lives. I had something to hope for.

When we were first living together, in Mark's tiny cottage in Wales, we used to listen to the tawny owls when we lay in bed. Mark could do an excellent tawny-owl impression. Now, I heard the owls on my own when I walked by the canal. Mark heard only the traffic from the main road. Even if he heard an owl, he could not get to the window to look for it. My career had ground to a halt, I was exhausted, I was furious, but, yes, I suppose I was lucky. My future was opaque, but at least I hoped to have one.

But, here's the thing: me, too. Mark was not dying *instead* of me; he was just dying *before* me. I still have this to come. One day, I will have to make that crossing back into the timelessness I came from, and so will everyone else. It will not feel like I have had a long enough turn. I hope, as many of us do, that my death, when it comes, will be quick and not preceded by months or years of pain. It is entirely possible that I will go with dementia. My family, after all, has form in that respect. More than 12 per cent of deaths in the UK are now from dementia, and many of those who die from other causes have dementia as well. Since 2015, it has been the leading cause of death in the UK. It is not improbable that I will suffer a long, slow, stripping away of my own self, like my mother, who was at first heartbreakingly aware of what she was losing, and later only a nonsensical bag of organs, incapable of any complexity of expression or thought. You were dying, Mark, but so are we all, sooner or later. And there was this, too: I was spending my precious, healthy, living years taking you through your end years, which was not how you spent your forties.

In 2019, an estimated 8.8 million adults in the UK were carers. No precise figure is possible, firstly because the number changes constantly as people become carers or cease to be carers, but also because it is not always easy to say exactly where a relationship tips from care, of the sort that people try to show their partners or parents anyway, to being 'a carer'. Around three in five people will be carers at some point in their lives. Most care in this country is provided by family and friends. Without it, our social services and health service would collapse. Carers are more likely to be women than men, about sixty/forty, and the peak age for caring is between fifty and sixty-four. About 40 per cent of carers look after a parent, and around a quarter look after a spouse or partner. Carers have worse health and less money than the general population. Forty per cent of them have not had a day off from caring in more than a year. Although one in two carers are also in paid work, more than half of all carers have had to give up work or reduce their hours. They are seven times more likely than non-carers to say they feel lonely all or most of the time.

When I googled 'becoming a carer', I found page after page of information about how to claim any benefits I might be entitled to. Important stuff, but I had hoped for something that would speak more to my experience. 'Emotional impact of becoming a carer' produced websites about fatigue, which definitely did resonate with me, but these accounts were nearly all scaffolded by a narrative that built the caring experience on love and worry for the person cared for, and focused on reassuring people that they were doing a good job. It seemed I was the only selfish and resentful carer out there, fearing the erosion of my own prospects and happiness, the only one for whom the worry was not that I was making a poor fist of being a carer, but that I was resentful about having to do this job at all. The belief shared by all the health professionals we met, by all the websites, by all my civilian friends was that carers are glad to care, because of love. Carers want to care; they have made a choice to do so. There is no place in that story for resentment, for feeling confined by a set of expectations you never agreed to, for feeling angry, overlooked and invisible. This is a convenient belief to hold. If unpaid family carers were not happy to care for their relatives, if it turned out that they did not find it an honour and a joy to be able to carry out such a service, it would make for an uncomfortable reckoning. It would mean that, as a society, we build our ability to function on a foundation of unhappiness. It means that each life compromised by illness, infirmity, misery or incapacity takes another life, at least temporarily, with it.

It helped me then, at least for a while, to refer to my own inner balance sheet. On one side, all the grounds I had for self-pity: Mark, my mother, the state of the house, my apparently wrecked career, the social isolation and the lack of practical support. On the other, all the 'at leasts': I was, myself, healthy, and so were the children; we had enough money, so long as I did not think about the costs of a care home for Mark; the children were no longer babies; my mother's needs were now being met by the staff of her residential home. Debits and credits. It was not great, but it could have been worse. Later, after Mark died, I met other young widows for whom it was worse: husbands who left huge debts, or whose unexpected mistresses came forward to contest the will. One woman had a seven-year-old daughter who was diagnosed with an aggressive cancer only a few months after her husband's death. Some bereaved spouses had been subject to personal abuse and harassed through the courts by their in-laws, who, in their own pain, were lashing out at anyone whom they might hold responsible; other anguished widows had lost their jobs because their employers could not tolerate more than a week or so of compassionate leave. I understood then that, in the hidden world of people who have been widowed young and with children, I was one of the lucky ones.

12

THE BLUE PIG

I was not alone in my hunger for friendship. Greg had moved to his new primary school halfway through his final year. He would be joining Adam at secondary school that September. Unlike his older sister and brother, Greg was quiet at school and preferred to have one or two close friends than to be part of a crowd. Would he be able to make friends at his new school? He had been somewhat adrift for the last few months in Melton, since his best friend Jaimil was deported back to India with his family. The dawning of Greg's political consciousness dates to this event and the realization that the policy decisions of Theresa May as Home Secretary had real and life-changing consequences for people he knew and loved. He had found no real replacement for Jaimil at his Melton school; would he be luckier at the Grantham one?

When I went to collect Greg after his first day at the new school, I felt confident that he would have coped well with the work, but was anxious to hear whether he had made any friends. He told me he had sat next to a small, clever boy called Edward, whom he thought might be his new best friend.

'He really loves space and stars and things. He's got a Chinese mum and a kind of Chinese face, and he looks like he's gone a bit mad with the blusher.' Just then, a woman and a boy came cycling past us, both bundled up in scarves and big coats. The child had pink cheeks and a delicate face under his bike helmet, and a fringe of black hair. 'That's him!'

I hoped this alliance between two nerdy ten-year-olds would last. There had been quite a risk, over those few years, in inviting any of the kids' friends to our house. Mark could be rude to or about any visitors to the home, so any socializing had to be carefully managed. His spell in hospital through January and February allowed Adam and Greg to bring school friends home for tea, cementing those new relationships, and meant that Rachel could invite her boyfriend to stay for a few days during her university reading week. Good. I was learning to appreciate how valuable strong friendships can be; sometimes a supportive friend feels more necessary than a marriage.

Our wedding anniversary is the 22 April. I just had to look that up. It is not a date I remember, and our wedding was so out of the ordinary, not at all the kind of wedding I had hoped for, early on in our relationship. After the first few weeks of our time together, Mark was almost studiously unromantic. He never told me again that he loved me. He did not generally believe in marriage, he told me: 'I see no reason why I need the Church or the state to sanction my relationship.' But he did suggest marriage once, in 2002, when I became pregnant – either with Adam or the time before, the one I lost. I cannot remember exactly. We were in the living room of my house in Leicester, one evening. I was standing by the window, looking out at the street, and Mark was behind the table at the other end of the room. He said, 'Stay there, because I don't want you to get the wrong idea. This is not meant to be romantic. Do you think we should maybe get married? I'm only saying this because of the baby.'

I felt like I had been punched, but I said nothing. Still now, I do not know why I thought I had to conceal from him how hurt and humiliated I felt. Would it be so terrible for him to show that he cared for me, was committed to me? At the time, my pride would not let me accept such a proposal. And, in the end, he got his unromantic wedding. This time, again, it was his idea, and this time, again, it was not motivated by love, but part of a project to set his affairs in order.

By this point in our relationship, I had stopped hoping for, or even wanting, romance. I was seriously thinking, in fact, that, if he were ever well enough to manage on his own, this might be the end of our partnership. Love and hurt had turned to bitterness and rage. To get married at that stage, when our relationship had never been worse, seemed an insane idea. When I told Rachel what we planned, as I was driving her home from university for the Easter holiday, she found it hard to understand why two people at the nadir of their relationship would contemplate matrimony. 'It's the maddest thing I've ever heard,' she said.

It took a month or so for Mark to talk me round, and never was there a stranger or less romantic wedding. Because he was, when he came home again, essentially bedridden, I needed to arrange for the registrar to come to our house, which required more forms to be completed and a note from the doctor. We assembled a wedding, of sorts, around Mark's bed.

On the day, I did the Asda shop in the morning. The registrar was coming at two o'clock, and I had asked my friend Diane and her partner to come and be witnesses. After I had made lunch for Mark and me, and tidied up, I cleaned the bathroom and brushed my hair. When everyone arrived, I was not sure of the protocol.

'Shall I make us a cup of tea, or should we just get on with it?'

The registrar thought there would be time for tea first, so we had a drink and a bit of small talk, and then we got married, with me sitting on the edge of Mark's bed. No dress, no photographer – indeed, no photographs – no brides-maids, no guests, no reception, no first dance and no cake, unless you count the malt loaf I had bought that morning from Asda. Then Diane and her partner left to inspect a slurry pit near Newark, a job they needed to do for work, and, a few minutes after that, Adam and Greg came home from school. That was that. I was Mark's wife – though, as it transpired, only for fifteen days, after which I turned into his widow.

Ten or twelve years earlier, I would have been delighted to marry Mark for love. By the time we finally did it, there was no romance left and the love we had was starved and weed-choked. But Mark was right. In a matter of weeks, I was spending my days on the phone, sorting out his insurance, his pension, his tax affairs and his probate. For all those things, it was so much easier that we had been married. Three weeks later, the registrar who had married us sent me a letter of condolence when she saw Mark's name entered on the register of deaths. 'We don't do many weddings like that,' she said, 'so I remembered you at once and was deeply affected to realize what had happened.' I knew that, to the registrar, I must look like a tragic deathbed bride, but I felt strangely disengaged from the whole process, as though, for a time, I was not the emotional architect of my own life.

One of the regular discussion points on the widows' internet forums, and wherever widows meet, is how friends who wept at the funeral have subsequently fallen silent and have never called or visited again. I have a few of those – and I do not blame them at all. I am sure I have let friendships drift myself, and you cannot always keep everyone in your life, especially when you live far away and have your own pressures. The other side of this coin, though, is that a period of prolonged and profound adversity shows you the kindness, steadiness and generosity of people whom you might not previously have expected to be your closest friends.

My friend Sarah was – and remains – just this kind of ally. We had been good friends at university and had kept in occasional touch in the years after. But, since the start of Mark's illness, we had been emailing and writing – Sarah is the only person I know who still writes proper letters which come in an envelope with a stamp on – with increasing frequency. In the five months between our move to Grantham and Mark's death, she came to visit twice from her home in Scotland, despite the distance and having her own family and job, with all the usual complications.

The evening of the day Mark and I were married, it was Sarah who came to visit for the weekend, turning up rumpled, late and grinning on Friday evening, having made the long train journey from Falkirk after work, and it was Sarah with whom I sat up late into the night. The decades of jobs and family and children had faded Sarah's hair from the flame red it had been in our student days, and both of us had baggier jawlines and droopier skin, but she was still beautiful in her home-knitted jumper, charity-shop boots and an Indian-looking tunic of the kind you might buy at a folk festival. We ate cheese on toast and drank a bottle of wine that made us sleepy. It grew late and we grew even more tired, but we could not quite leave each other to head for bed, even though our eyelids felt like they had weights on them.

Next morning, Sarah woke up feeling vigorous and practical. The huge and overgrown garden at the new house was making me despair. I had neither the time, inclination, nor the skill to start work on it, but, with Sarah's encouragement and vitality, I found myself, to my surprise, enjoying the process of slashing and chopping at the snowberries that were usurping the driveway. Undaunted by the size and apparent futility of the task, Sarah began weeding and sweeping the paths and patio. Accomplishing something – anything – boosted my mood and morale as much as talking for hours about our shared memories, our current situations and future hopes did.

After lunch, Sarah came with me into town to collect Mark's prescription, and then, feeling light and liberated to be out of the house and in company, I suggested we go into a pub in town. Despite living in Grantham for five months, I had not been into any of the pubs, and there are some interesting ones: the Beehive, which had an actual beehive in a tree outside the door instead of a pub sign, for example, or the Nobody Inn, which always seemed to be packed, or the lovely medieval Blue Pig, opposite the church. We chose the Blue Pig, that Saturday afternoon, and sat at a table by the small, leaded window, with our halves of bitter. It felt like twenty-five years ago, wasting hours in the pubs of Cambridge, when we were students.

'Do you remember the night we decided to swim home, and we jumped into the Cam at Midsummer Common, only in our underwear and T-shirts, and how muddy we got when we clambered onto the bank by the Fen Causeway, and had to walk home soaking wet and bare-legged?'

'Or the excavation in Thessaly, with a bunch of Dutch students who distinguished us by calling us Sarah Redhead and Sarah Blackhead?'

It felt good to be reminded of a person I used to be, of the people we used to be: people who loved to swim and dance and sing the wrong words to silly pop songs in the kitchen.

Tipsy with memories of other selves, and with having had a pint of Landlord each, we arrived home to start on dinner. I went to check on Mark and bring him a cup of tea. We had a short conversation, but I was dying to get back to

Sarah downstairs, because I was having such a good time. We were chopping vegetables, listening to music and mucking around, laughing in the kitchen, when Mark called me up to his room. As soon as I got there, I could see how upset he was. Furious, he set about me in hurt and anger: did we find it funny that he was up here, dying alone? How could I ignore or forget his suffering? What was I thinking, to go off drinking and laughing, leaving behind a man who could not follow us? It was abandonment and it was cruel.

I had nothing to say. My life was neither fun nor easy, and I felt that I deserved a break and to spend time alone with my friend, but, however difficult my life was at that time, it was so much better than his. I felt the justice of his rage. Why were we gossiping together downstairs, rather than sitting in his room and relieving his isolation and boredom? There was no good reason, or nothing I could say to him. The truth was that I wanted respite, that Sarah was my friend rather than his, that he was bad-tempered and difficult company and not a pleasant person to spend time with. But all he could hear were the sounds of happiness from somewhere he was not – indeed, from somewhere he could not reach, either physically or mentally – and it must have felt like, at best, indifference to his pain. I tried to apologize, to reassure him, but felt chastened and guilty. The rest of the evening was subdued. Sarah and I came up together and sat by Mark's bed, but he was too ill, hurt and angry for an easy chat, and we felt too chastised to find again the euphoria of the afternoon. Mark wanted me to go to him for companionship, fun and emotional support, not to a friend, but, at a time of relentless stress, and when our relationship was itself a cause of that stress, I desperately needed those other anchors.

As soon as I got up the following day, I went to check on Mark. Normally, I would make him a cup of tea and bring his morning medication, which he took while I emptied his catheter bag and brought him a flannel for his hands and face. But that morning he looked at me, stricken, and said, 'Thank God you're up. I've been in agony.'

His catheter tube had somehow been pulled half out during the night, leaving him in terrible pain. It needed reinserting and neither of us could manage it. At 7.30, I called for a nurse, who said she would not be able to get to us before 10.30 a.m. In the meantime, the painkillers seemed to have little effect and Mark was distressed. I was aware that my friend had come from Scotland to be with me that weekend, and I was failing as a hostess. I could hear her clattering about in the kitchen, presumably getting her own breakfast, since I was not doing it, but I could not leave Mark. The children would have to fend for themselves. It is frustrating and upsetting to see somebody in pain and be unable to make things any better, though undoubtedly better than being the person in pain. I brought useless cups of tea and tried layering paracetamol on top of the ibuprofen, but nothing seemed to touch his hurt.

Eventually, after two district nurses had tried and failed, it seemed that Mark would need to go to the hospital so that somebody there could get the tube back in – under anaesthetic, if necessary – so we called an ambulance. At this stage in his illness, Mark's disability was so severe that I could not get him to the car. He needed to be carried downstairs. We needed paramedics to get him from his bed to the hospital. It was lunchtime before they arrived, but, when we got to A and E, we were seen quite quickly, and the emergency urologist, a cheerful Nigerian doctor, managed to position the tube without difficulty. There then followed a considerable period of wheedling by me to arrange for some help getting him back home and into bed.

Realizing that the chances of me having time to talk or dig the garden were slim, Sarah took an early train home around the same time that the ambulance came. She had been with us less than forty-eight hours, and spent less than half of that time with me, but the impact of her visit on my mood was colossal. I had a friend, and she was worth more to me than all the banana boards in the world. During the next few months, we all came to depend on those steady and deep relationships. In the years since Mark's death, I have made new friends, including Edward's mother, who had cycled past us on Greg's first day at his Grantham school, but those old friends who saw me at my worst and stayed by me feel like arms around my shoulders that have kept me – and still keep me – from stumbling, and steady me when I do. Six years later, Greg and Edward are still best friends.

That, then, was the last time that Mark saw Sarah. He had already, at that point, seen his sister for the last time, and nearly all of his friends. It is funny – you always remember firsts: how you first met somebody important to you, your first visit to a new place. In a relationship, you remember your first kiss, the first time you had sex. But it is rare that you feel as weightily the significance of lasts. I do not even know which lasts have already passed for me. Some I am sure of: I have had my last child, I will never breastfeed again. Will I ever do another long run? I have, in my life, run marathons, all of them glacially slow and hard to finish, but I pushed on and managed to shuffle, sponge-legged, across the finish line. Have I already run my last marathon? My last half-marathon? I am not running nearly as much, these days. I stopped entirely during the last couple of years of Mark's life, when I realized that going for a run was no longer something relaxing and had slipped somehow into being another chore to feel guilty about not doing. Normally, you do not know at the time that this is the last occasion you will see somebody before they die, or that this is the last time in your life you will travel in a train, or go to the supermarket. You do not know that this will be the last time you have sex with this partner – or, at some point, with anyone at all – or the last time you take somebody a cup of tea. I wonder if Mark thought about those last things, if he knew the date his life would end. Did he think, That's the last time I leave the house, or, That will be the last episode of *The News Quiz* I hear? Was he even then planning, like Sydney Carton, his extraordinary act of sacrifice, telling nobody the whole shape of his plan?

13

PROBABLY ONE, BUT WE'LL NEVER KNOW FOR SURE

How many archaeologists does it take to change a lightbulb? Probably one, but we'll never know for sure. It is a joke, but also, not entirely a joke. Archaeologists, more than anyone, are used to not knowing. We only ever have best guesses, plausible stories, maybes and possiblys. Given the scarcity of unequivocal answers in archaeology, and given that I have always embraced complexity and uncertainty in my academic life, I was surprised that I found the inconclusive and open-ended nature of Mark's diagnosis so hard to handle.

In public life, vagueness, ambiguity and room for doubt are scorned as proof of failure, incompetence or lack of backbone. Certainty is all. 'Is it true or isn't it?' shout the journalists on the radio. But we know that science does not always produce truth. At best, it gives us facts; how we organize the facts into stories is open to discussion. If our archaeological data are underdetermined, incomplete and ambiguous – or, sometimes, bogglingly complicated – there is always space to tell other stories, to weave different patterns. But we should not necessarily see the nature of our evidence as a problem. In fact, it echoes more truly the messy and complicated nature of the lost lives, relationships and processes we try to explain. In other words, even if we somehow had all the facts there are, we would still not have a final unambiguous story about the past. If I stand outside on a clear night, I can see stars. I recognize some constellations: a lion, a plough, a hunter. But if I picked out only some of those stars and maybe included some from other parts of the sky, or if I was educated in a different kind of astronomy, I would make different constellations: a snake, a jug, a child. And if I were somewhere else in the galaxy, I would see some of the same stars, but none of the same patterns. I make my own story constellations from what I already know, and where I am, and what I expect to see.

The truth of the matter is that there is no truth of the matter. There are always other stories, other constellations. Not that this helped me at all to deal with the ambiguity of Mark's condition. Which story were we in? One where he got better or one where he died? A romance? A tragedy? A whodunnit? In any case, it all looks different from the part of the galaxy I am in now.

The first diagnosis Mark received, tentative and incomplete as it was, was autoimmune encephalitis. That still did not give us a cause. Encephalitis is just a way of describing inflammation in the brain, something that was clear from his first scans. Encephalitis described *what* was happening in Mark's head, but not *why* it was happening. The doctor's initial hope was that Mark's epileptic seizures had caused a small amount of damage to the brain, and that, once the seizures stopped, the brain – a remarkably plastic organ, which can often make good any damage, if the rest of the body is healthy – would heal. That did not happen. Instead, over time, the area affected was slowly expanding. The seizures, it seemed, were an effect and not a cause of whatever was happening in Mark's head. Encephalitis is usually either infectious or autoimmune. Infectious cases tend to come on suddenly and worsen rapidly. Autoimmune encephalitis can be slower to develop and harder to diagnose. In that case, antibodies produced by your own body attack the brain. Medical understanding of autoimmune encephalitis is advancing rapidly, and new antibodies are being discovered all the time to add to the register of those known to be associated with encephalitis. Mark was tested for the most common ones at Leicester, and then at Nottingham. Every test came back negative.

The third possible cause of encephalitis is paraneoplastic – the indirect result of a cancer somewhere in the body. As with the other autoimmune forms, it is caused by an over-zealous immune response. With paraneoplastic encephalitis, the body might have been very effective in fighting a cancer, which could be so small the patient was not even aware of it, but goes on to attack healthy tissue, sometimes even after the cancer has disappeared. Mark had two full-body scans to see if any cancer could be detected by visual imaging, and a series of blood tests to look for markers of the most likely kinds of cancer. Again, these kept drawing blanks. However, Mark had very slightly raised levels of alphafetoprotein, which can be associated with testicular cancer, and detailed scans of his testicles showed a slight shadow. To be on the safe side, and to check whether he might have had a cancerous tumour there which had resolved on its own, the urologist at Leicester decided to remove the testicle.

Years before, after Gregory was born, Mark and I had agreed that we did not want any more children. I had always taken responsibility for contraception in our relationship. I have noted, in many of the men I know, an unbecoming pride in never visiting the doctor and not needing prescriptions for anything, and Mark was no different. Somewhat resentfully, I was aware, first, that this scrupulousness about using medication did not extend to anything acquired illegally or that was not properly tested, and, second, that the cost of keeping his body pure and natural was to dope mine up with synthetic hormones, and for me to take responsibility for all the medical visits and prescription collections that involved. But, after Gregory's birth, Mark said that he had no objection to getting a vasectomy, except that he found the idea of being cut unpleasant. He was nevertheless prepared, he assured me, to make a decision 'in principle' to get the snip. But a decision in principle was not going to be effective as a family-planning strategy. I went back to the clinic and got a coil.

I might have felt a grim satisfaction, then, that the temple of Mark's body was now a pharmacopoeia, and that the man who refused to have a minor procedure nine years earlier was now facing the excision of a testicle. But Mark was so morose, it was impossible not to feel sorry for him. The night before the operation, Mark suggested we have sex, 'to say goodbye to it'. It had been months since we had been intimate. I did not want him even to touch me, or to see me naked. Every night, I climbed carefully into my side of the bed, wearing my most voluminous nightgown, careful not to touch him. I was a grenade of cold fury, with tripwires that stretched from the kitchen to the living room, to the bed. I had never wanted physical contact less.

When we went to see the urologist a few weeks later, it crossed my mind that Mark was probably the only person in that waiting room hoping to be told that he had cancer. If he had cancer, his encephalitis could be confirmed as paraneoplastic, the cancer could be treated, and he would have a good chance of getting better. Testicular cancer is one of the more curable kinds, with a 98 per cent five-year survival rate. If there is a 'good' cancer to get, this is it. However, there was no evidence that Mark did have cancer, nor that he had ever had it. Not paraneoplastic, then.

In the last few years of his life, Mark probably consumed ten times as much medication as he had during all the rest of his life up to that point. At the time Mark started to have symptoms, our medicine cabinet was meagre and infrequently opened, except for plasters and Calpol for the kids – and the odd sneaky swig of Calpol for me, during the sleep-deprived addle of the children's baby and toddler years.

As soon as Mark's seizures were identified as epilepsy, he was put on one of the standard epilepsy drugs, Keppra (levetiracetam), twice a day. Although this helped reduce the number of seizures, he was still having several episodes a day, so another antiepileptic, lamotrigine, was added to the Keppra.

Then, as his physical condition worsened, he was given steroids, at first intravenously and then orally, in very large doses. So his daily medication now included, as well as the epilepsy drugs and antidepressants, prednisolone, the steroid; omeprazole, to protect his stomach from damage by the steroid; carbamazepine, intended to reduce the severity of his other neurological symptoms, such as itching and pain; Adcal, to reduce the chances of the steroids causing osteoporosis; co-trimoxazole, an antibiotic to combat his chronic urinary-tract infections; fluconazole, to protect against fungal infections that might result from his antibiotic use; and amlodipine and low-dose aspirin, for his blood pressure, which was on the high side, anyway, and had been made worse since his illness prevented him from getting proper exercise.

As well as the regular daily medications, Mark's doctors tried a buffet of other treatments necessitating hospital admission. He had several rounds of plasma exchange, which would – temporarily, anyway – wash his blood of any circulating antibodies that might be attacking his brain. His first plasma-exchange treatment had a marked effect on his mood and his physical abilities for a couple of weeks at least, though the second treatment was less effective than the first, and subsequent treatments had progressively smaller and briefer effects.

He was then given a series of infusions of cyclophosphamide, usually used as part of chemotherapy for cancers, but, because it suppresses the immune system, Dr Leite thought it might have a beneficial effect on Mark. He had to make regular trips to Oxford so that he could be plugged into a machine, and he quite enjoyed the change of scene, chatting with the nurses, going for a cup of tea and an egg roll afterwards in the WRVS cafeteria. The cyclophosphamide, however, had no effect at all.

Modern medical science is a wonderful thing. The diagnostic tools available to doctors today and the variety of effective treatment options are way ahead of where we were just a few decades ago, even for diseases that were previously considered untreatable. And when the best drugs fail to save us, there are palliative-care drugs that are supposed to let us ease away from life, allow us to cease upon the midnight with no pain. What I know now is that, though we may put our faith in pharmacology, drugs will sometimes let us down; though we know a lot, we do not know everything, and we are very bad at saying, or hearing, 'We do not know how to make this better.' And we are very bad at supplying the community, the human contact, that would compensate for the things that our science and technology cannot do.

In *Every Third Thought*, Robert McCrum attributes his generation's difficulty dealing with mortality to an overinvestment in the independent, active self, always capable of and entitled to the pursuit of self-fulfilment. He and his friends are people who have been raised to believe that they have the power themselves to find or create exactly the life they want, to claim the life they deserve. If there is a problem, willpower and the right strategy can sort it out. You can be anything you want. Except, disappointingly, immortal. Such boomer confidence is not easily reconciled to aging, dependency, decline and ultimately, inevitably, death. McCrum has a few years on me, but my generation is no different. For us, too, the medical profession colludes in the comfortable lie that there is Something To Be Done, and that, with determination and the right drugs, we can vanquish the creeping tumours, the brain plaques, the choked heart and the ruptured artery. We are thus not so well equipped, says McCrum, to face up to death and decline as previous generations were. What used to be an unavoidable truth, to be addressed stoically and with all the consolations that faith and philosophy could supply, is now to be looked at obliquely or not at all. The eager, seventeenth-century consumers of *ars moriendi* books knew something that too many of us have forgotten.

In cases of neurological illness, all the recent talk of brain plasticity contributes to our collective fantasy that things can usually be fixed. Our friend Simon is one of the most optimistic people I know. A confident and ambitious New Zealander, Simon pushes ahead with whatever plan or dream comes to his mind. Most recently, he has invested all his savings and resources in a tract of land in New South Wales to make an avocado farm, though he is already over seventy and has a dodgy foot, and it takes at least seven years before a newly planted avocado tree can be expected to yield a marketable crop. Simon is the embodiment of can-do, the most buoyant and enthusiastic of men. During Mark's last year, Simon had read a book by psychiatrist Norman Doidge, *The Brain's Way of Healing*, in which Doidge explains neuroplasticity, the discovery that the human brain can recover function, and even regenerate damaged structure, if given the right kind of therapy. This is true, says Doidge, even for many people suffering from conditions previously thought to be irreversible. Simon was sure that this book would give Mark reason to hope, and was eager that Mark should read it too, and take both inspiration and practical help from the case studies, treatments and exercises. He had been planning to bring it over the week Mark died – and, after his death, regretted his delay. I think he really believed that Doidge's insights could have prevented Mark's death, but I cannot see how, given the duration and severity of the damage Mark endured. Neuroplasticity offers real benefit to many people whose lives have been constrained and reduced by conditions and symptoms, but plasticity is not the same as unlimited regenerative power and, at some point, treatments cannot prevent all neurological diseases from progressing. Not everyone can be cured.

During the last year of his life, Mark reconnected with his ex-wife, Hilary. Theirs had been a short-lived marriage, which unravelled when they both had affairs at around the same time, only a few months after they had tied the knot. Maybe this was part of the reason he had not wanted to marry me. It had, however, been a relatively amicable parting, which had taken place years before I even met him. She had gone on to remarry, have four children and then have another relationship after that.

In the spring of 2016, Hilary had cause to be driving frequently between London and Manchester, and was able, at least twice, to break her journey in Oxford to visit Mark while he was having inpatient treatment there. I only met her once before Mark's funeral, about three weeks before he died, when she came to visit him at our house. I was pleased she had come. Mark's life was so tiny then, played out entirely in his bed, with only the boys and me to punctuate his day, and the radio for company. There was an element, too, of personal curiosity to meet this woman who had once been Mark's great love. After so many years together, I was past the point of being jealous of Mark's exes, but I wondered, would she be like me? Did Mark have a type?

She arrived – slimmer, richer, older than me, but stylish, confident and direct. I could see how he would like that. The conversation turned, as it often did, around Mark's illness. Hilary was not one of those who saw the ongoing absence of a clear diagnosis of his condition as a personal challenge (I had one colleague at the university, for example, who always had suggestions for new avenues to be explored, despite his lack of any medical training or experience. He used to greet me by saying things like, 'Sarah! Good morning! Have you thought of Lyme disease?'). Hilary was, however, excited to hear that Mark's consultant thought his illness might be autoimmune. As it happens, she enthused, her partner had also been suffering from an autoimmune problem – only, in his case, it had been successfully treated and entirely cured, following Hilary's own research, by the daily consumption of a vitamin-B supplement. She thought such a regime might also work for Mark, and had taken the liberty, if it was all right, of bringing a bottle of vitamin tablets with her, which she placed on his bedside cabinet, as if setting a Fabergé egg on a velvet cushion. I policed my face. Really? I thought. He has been seen by half a dozen senior neurologists in three counties, and you think they have all missed a simple vitamin deficiency?

Apart from irritation at the arrogance of the move, I have trouble now remembering what made me so cross. False hope it might have been, but where is the harm in that? Mark must have known how unlikely such quackery was to have any benefit, but he took the pills anyway. I would have done the same. As Terry Pratchett, the prolific satirist and author of scores of humour and fantasy novels, said of some of the New Age remedies that were suggested for his incurable Alzheimer's disease, 'I'd eat the arse out of a dead mole if it offered a fighting chance.' Maybe it was Hilary's failure to recognize the severity of Mark's condition that irked me. He was not under the weather. He was not one of those who are frequently diagnosed with a non-specific autoimmune condition after complaining of rather vague symptoms, and who, in all investigations, appear normal. Mark's scan and test results were dramatically abnormal; we just did not know what was causing the abnormalities. He was paralysed, incontinent, his senses profoundly affected. I had never met Hilary's partner, but I was willing to bet that his autoimmune condition was nothing like Mark's – like comparing a nasty blister to an amputated leg. Inwardly, I raged against the bracketing of Mark's situation with that of this unknown man. I wanted her to be realistic, to acknowledge what was happening, what was bound to happen, and she was instead exemplifying McCrum's point about her generation: for her, the approach of death was a problem to be solved, a threat to be avoided.

Questions of what makes a good or bad death preoccupy McCrum, a man in middle age and aware of the inevitable finish of the out-of-control, downhill tumble we are on. He is a master of the memento mori, a rather neglected topic of art and culture that was ubiquitous in the early modern world and now is seldom seen and even more seldom taken seriously. However, there are still occasions when we could do with the reminder. All this focus on cure only defers the inevitable emotional impact of knowing that we too will die. Memento mori. All this has to stop sometime.

My friend Richard is a computer scientist who has worked on projects ranging from the Mars rover to the safe decommissioning of oil wells and the organization of clinical trials. One of the projects he was involved in a few years ago dealt with the treatment of people with Alzheimer's disease. Richard introduced me to the QALY – Quality-Adjusted Life Year. The QALY is a way of putting a value on the benefit of medical interventions. A year of perfect health equals one QALY. Death has a score of zero. A year spent alive but in imperfect health has a score of between zero and one. There are no negative QALYs. Considering the cost of a medical treatment against the benefit, measured in QALYs, is supposed to help people make clinical decisions about what treatments are worthwhile, and the best allocation of limited public funding. For example, if a patient has a chronic condition that reduces their quality of life to 0.5, and a treatment comes along that would ease their symptoms sufficiently to give them a QALY of 0.75, without any effect on their overall life expectancy, that would be a QALY gain of 0.25 a year. If a patient had a condition that did not make their daily quality of life much worse – a QALY of 0.8, for example – but meant their life expectancy was only two years, and a new drug became available that would extend their life to four years, without affecting their quality of life, they would gain 1.6 – that is, 0.8 times the two additional years. Typically, medical use of the phrase 'quality of life' means life without serious pain and in which one can still do ordinary things. It does not slip into the metaphysics of what makes a life meaningful or what it is worth being alive for.

When I was about ten, we were on a family camping holiday in northern France. I spent most of my days playing on the beach with my sister and brother. I remember being fascinated by the little keel worms whose feathery tentacles emerged into the shallow water of the rock pools. It struck me how strangely restricted their lives were – waiting for the tide to come in, and then swaying in the water, catching bits of food for a few hours, retreating back into their holes, and then repeating the whole business again, twelve hours later. For their whole lives. Until they died of whatever keel worms die of, or were eaten by gulls or fish or crabs or something. What was the point? Were they even happy? I shared my thoughts with Dad. His response was not comforting.

'What's the point in any of our lives?'

This was scary. Was my life just another version of the

keel worm's? All the playing and going to school, the eating, reading, watching telly – were they just so much tentacle-waving? The going to sleep and waking up, and putting my clothes on and taking them off again. Was I just filling in the time before a giant metaphorical seagull gobbled me up?

I have not resolved the question of what makes a good or meaningful life, unfortunately, but I am fairly sure that there has to be more to it than just waving my tentacles around for a span, without being in major pain. The problem with QALYs is that all they take into account is degree of suffering or impairment, and time. The worth of a life can be measured as a function of those two things, and a low score in one variable can be compensated by a higher score in the other. So, if your experience of being alive is really pretty awful – pain, for example, and mental anguish, immobility and sensory deprivation, all at once – you could have a very low QALY score of 0.1. But, according to the formula, it would be possible to make up for that by extending life expectancy for more years. So, ten years in those dreadful circumstances would be equivalent to one really great year of full health, swimming with dolphins, eating ice cream and generally enjoying all that your sturdy body allowed. Taking a horrible situation and making it last longer is not what most people would think of as reasonable compensation.

Terry Pratchett died in 2015, aged sixty-six, having written at least seventy-five books. This is all the more remarkable an output considering that, for the last eight years of his life, he was suffering from incurable dementia, specifically posterior cortical atrophy, a form of early-onset Alzheimer's disease. Nobody ever comes back from PCA. All you can do is barricade yourself inside the castle with as much heavy furniture piled up against the door as you can assemble, and hope that it takes a long time for the battering ram belonging to the murderous and implacable army that is laying siege to your brain to break through. And this is no movie: there is no cavalry to save you in the nick of time; the castle will fall.

Pratchett thought hard, as you would, about what to do when that time approaches. If he were able to recognize the splintering of the door or its irrecoverable unhinging, what would he want? Possessed, as Mark was not, of a terminal diagnosis, Pratchett was able to begin the process of arranging a trip to the Swiss euthanasia clinic operated by Dignitas. In the end, he did not take this trip, though he was a passionate advocate of choosing the time and manner of one's own death, which he believed was a profoundly sane choice. Although the traditional assessment of suicide was that it happened when the balance of one's mind was temporarily disturbed, 'I've reached the conclusion,' he said, 'that a person may make a decision to die because the balance of their mind is level, realistic, pragmatic, stoic and sharp. And that is why I dislike the term "assisted suicide" applied to the carefully thought-out and weighed-up process of having one's life ended by gentle medical means.'

If he could be sure that his end was in his own control, the days, weeks, months or years leading up to it would be made not only less fearful, but more precious. In a lecture he gave in 2010, Pratchett finished by saying, 'I would like to die peacefully, with Thomas Tallis on my iPod, before the disease takes me over, and I hope that will not be for quite some time to come, because, if I knew that I could die at any time I wanted, then suddenly every day would be as precious as a million pounds. If I knew that I could die, I would live. My life, my death, my choice.'

Mark and I talked about death quite a bit. This was not new. Normally, I can talk easily to anyone about death – up until then, I had never found it an uncomfortable subject or worried that I would say the wrong thing. The anthropologist Geoffrey Gorer claimed in 1965 that death had become taboo, that nobody was able to talk with him, or let him talk about the death of his brother, even though it affected him deeply. But this was never my experience: I do not feel awkward around bereaved people, nor have I ever felt unable to talk about my own grief. I found the limits of my conversational ease, though, in talking with Mark about his own forthcoming end. The discussions we had as his symptoms became more severe and the assurances that he would get better stopped coming were untethered and strange, both of us shy of upsetting the other one. Why was this so different? I think it was because we were afraid of admitting that we thought his death was imminent. Previously, I had been used to talking about certain facts: somebody had died, in specific circumstances, and nobody would be upset by me stating that; there was no comfortable, or uncomfortable, illusion to be maintained. As an archaeologist, and as a funeral celebrant, I was accustomed to looking back at the event from the far side, not eyeing it up in front of me. Talking about a probable forthcoming death with the person who is facing it, and being tangled up in a personal relationship with that person, is altogether different from both academic discussions of historical trends or archaeological evidence, and from talking to the bereaved about their loss. This death, if and when it comes, will affect me more profoundly than any other I have experienced – more than the death of my father or of any of the friends, colleagues and acquaintances whose lives have already ended. The longer Mark's illness went on, and the more symptoms appeared, the more crystalline became my realization that this could end in his death. And yet none of the medical people we saw mentioned this possibility. Was I catastrophizing? Was Mark being melodramatic? He changed his profile picture on social media to a photograph of one of the skulls I had been studying for my research project. If he died . . . But I must not even think that. What kind of a monster plans for their partner's death? We both wanted permission to rehearse our thoughts, feelings, plans on the subject, and yet were scared of hurting each other, of being mistaken about the severity of his condition. When death had not been mentioned as a possibility, our trespassing imaginings felt out of bounds, even to each other. Four years after his first symptoms, with no clear sense of where we were in the landscape of life and death, and only our own observations of decline to give us a sense of our direction of travel, it would have been helpful to be told that he might die, and that, although nobody can say for certain, people with neurological conditions like Mark's often die within a year or two. Or within ten, or live out a natural lifespan and then die of something unrelated. Whichever. Our questions remained unasked and unanswered.

The last time the paramedics came before he died, it was because Mark had fallen from his bed and I could not lift him. Each time they attend a call, the paramedics need to fill out a report. This one was clearly not a major incident, but it looked like it might have major consequences for us.

'He shouldn't really be here, you know. It isn't safe.'

'I know. We really appreciate your help. But now I know how to get him back up if he falls again, and I'm sure our boys could help.'

'No. I mean, it's really not safe. What if there were a fire? How would you get him out? We have to report this.'

Their concerns were not entirely a surprise, and it was a possibility that we had talked about. He might need to move somewhere he could get proper care. A place that was set up for people with disabilities. A care home.

'Don't report us yet,' I pleaded. 'If you give us another few weeks, we will make our own arrangements, I promise. And next week we've planned for the registrar to come here so that we can get married. At least give us long enough for that to happen. I swear, we'll take steps after that.'

The paramedics looked doubtful, but we must have appealed to their sense of romance, or evoked their pity, because they agreed to our request for a short delay.

Two weeks later, I went to look at three care homes in our town. It was utterly miserable. My mother, whose dementia had by then advanced to the point at which she could no longer stay in her own home, was already in residential care. My sister Jo and I had visited quite a few homes before we chose Mum's, so I was familiar with the set-up. It felt quite different, though, to be looking for a place for Mark. The things I had wanted for Mum – sing-songs, games of bingo and carpet bowls, the company of dozens of other elderly women – were a grotesque living environment for a clever man of working age. All the residents were so much older than him, many with incipient dementia. The idea of wheeling him out every morning to be parked in front of a TV, or expecting him to join in with sing-songs from the war was appalling. He was still intellectually sharp, and only needed physical care. When I came out of the third home, I sat in the car with my head in my hands.

Why had I allowed us to buy this stupid, impractical house? Why did we not choose a normal, modern house on an estate, that we could adapt easily for him, so he could be looked after at home?

I took the brochures and price lists from the three care homes and spread them out that evening on the kitchen table. I said nothing to Mark. Our town is in one of the cheaper parts of England. Houses are cheap, and care-home rates are lower than average. Even so, we would be looking at around £50,000 a year, minimum. Mark's income from his pension was £18,000. I would need to find an extra £32,000 a year or more. I got out a notebook and listed all our assets. We would be OK for a little while, but we would run through our savings very quickly – and then what? A smaller house, of course, would release a bit more. On another page, I listed all our usual expenses and subtracted them from my take-home pay. Not nearly enough. Cancel all holidays, clothes and subscriptions. Reduce every other budget head by 10 per cent. Still not even close. And that was assuming I would be able to carry on working full-time, with nobody at home to help with the children. I had told Mark that, if and when the time came that he needed residential care, we would be able to manage. I was not prepared to tell him now that we could not, nor to let him know how much it was going to cost. We would be OK for a couple of years, anyway, I reckoned, and by then something would turn up. If not, I could ask my family. I would need to talk to him about moving into care, and we would have to have that conversation soon, but not today, not just yet. I could not face it, could not face him. I knew he would hate to be in any of the places I had visited, but I could not see any alternative to sentencing him to one of them. I felt like a traitor. I was a traitor.

14

INCOMMENSURABLE BELIEFS

The good thing about the continuing-bonds approach to bereavement is that it leaves space for grief to remain unresolved, for the bereaved to go on missing and loving the person who has died, and to gain legitimate comfort from a continued connection, whether that be by talking to the dead, investing their things with meaning, or including them in their conversations and plans. Less frequently discussed are those ongoing relationships that are characterized by negative and hostile emotions. History and archaeology are full of them. The dead can be the object of resentment, revenge, spite, prejudice and anger, as well as love and honour.

As a student, I was fascinated by the archaeological site of Balladoole on the Isle of Man. Excavated during the Second World War by Gerhard Bersu, a German archaeologist interned as an enemy alien on the island, the site contained a Norse boat burial, dating from around the year AD 900. The burial had rich grave goods, a substantial boat and the remains of animals and possibly at least one other person besides the main passenger on the ship. However, the pagan Norse were not the first to take advantage of this hilltop site. There were also Mesolithic, Bronze Age and Iron

Age features at the site, and the remains of an early Christian chapel. Most dramatically, immediately beneath the boat burial was a Christian cemetery with at least seventeen burials. To bury the boat, several of those earlier graves had been disturbed, and the decomposing bodies dragged out and left on the ground surface beneath the Norse boat. The hand and foot bones of the bodies that were moved were still articulated, which tells us that they had not been long enough in the ground for the ligaments holding them together to have decayed. Opinions differ as to what the Balladoole boat burial means, but I find it hard to interpret it as anything other than a hostile act, using the very bodies of the dead to pursue a conflict between Christian and pagan, between established population and newcomer.

Continuing-bonds theorists are right that strong emotions still link us to the dead, that dying does not end a relationship, but it is also true that those relationships are not always ones of affection and love. We survivors can have much nastier feelings about the dead too.

Since I first read about the Balladoole boat burial as a student, I have been fascinated by posthumous punishment, by the ways that the living act out their vengefulness, fury and spite on the bodies of the dead. This culminated for me in a five-year research project on what happened to the bodies of executed criminals in the eighteenth and nineteenth centuries AD, the well-funded project that ended up being totally eclipsed by the discovery of Richard III. By the middle of the eighteenth century, rampant inflation of punishment had taken hold in England and Wales. So many things were, in theory, punishable by death – including damaging the banks of a canal or writing poison pen letters, for example – that people started to look around for some even harsher punishment to mark out particularly nasty capital crimes. In continental Europe, ever more gruesome ways of putting somebody to death were designed to fulfil this purpose. In Britain, the solution was to extend punishment past the point of death. For this reason, in 1751, An Act for Better Preventing the Horrid Crime of Murder was passed. That Act ruled that the body of an executed murderer should not receive a normal Christian burial, but should instead either be passed to the anatomists for dissection, or be gibbeted. Gibbeting involved leaving the body hanging in a cage from a post, a tree or a purpose-built gibbet, until it fell to pieces and was consumed by animals and the natural processes of decay.

Why did anyone think that posthumous punishment was going to be an effective deterrent? Some people told me it was because a fragmented body could not be resurrected, that it was truly a punishment of the soul. But this is not what anyone said at the time, as far as I know. Quite the reverse, in fact. Both Catholic and Protestant writers were keen to stress God's ability to reconstruct a body for resurrection, even from the smallest and least promising pieces – like the scientists in Jurassic Park making a diplodocus from a drop of blood in a mosquito's belly. In the late seventeenth century, Oxford preacher Thomas Beconsall took a forensic approach to the mechanics of bodily resurrection, in which he concludes that God will reform the body out of whatever particles of it can be found, even 'those fleeting Particles . . . that are carried off by more nice and delicate sorts of Evacuation'. So, if there was no theological justification for using dissection as a punishment, why did people mind? All the writing of the period that I came across seemed to suggest they should not.

What did people really believe about the dead body in the early modern world? Thomas Becon, the author of *The Sicke Mannes Salve*, looked forward to when, 'so soone as my soule shall bee delivered out of the prison of this my body, it shall straight wayes possesse the blessed inheritance of the heavenly kingdome'. Fellow *ars moriendi* author Zacharie Boyd asked, in 1629, rhetorically, 'Is it not your greatest desire to flitte from this bodie which is but a Booth, a shoppe, or Tabernacle of clay? Is not your Soule wearie to sojourne into such a reekie Lodge?' The dead body is just food for worms; the life of the body, with its appetites, its lumpishness, its hungers and lusts, is totally opposed to the pure spirit. And death? It is a mocking reminder of the worthlessness of the flesh, a rebuke to our vanity. Alicia Woodforde, wife of the diarist Samuel Woodforde, died following the birth of her second child, in 1664. Because she was afraid of being buried alive, she had asked to be left in bed for two or three days before being laid out – not an unusual request at the time. But, after one day, her body smelled repugnant, and her stomach had swollen so badly that it had to be bound to stop it bursting. Her distraught husband reflected in his diary, 'Oh God, what things are wee when once thou callest for Our breath into thyne owne hands.'

Common to all these seventeenth-century writers is a more or less explicit contrast between the body and the soul. While the soul is eternal, glorious, divine, beautiful and pure, the body is changeable, material, ugly, earthen. Time and care spent on attending to the needs of the body are vain and futile.

But what I was seeing when I looked at the archaeological evidence from burials in this period did not fit this picture. Instead, there was a massive expenditure of care and effort on the dead body. The deceased was more likely than ever to be enclosed in a coffin or wax-impregnated cloth to impede decay, dressed in good clothes or in nightclothes, as if for bed. They were buried with their false teeth in and their hairpieces on, looking as good as they could, under the circumstances. They were buried with pretty and sweet-scented plants around their heads, and on their graves were elaborate memorials. Even as the theologians were emphasizing the meaninglessness of the dead body, people were increasingly choosing to be buried in the same grave as their spouse, children or parents. There was no lack of care for the body here, no rejection of meaning – rather an overabundance, if anything.

I started out by asking questions about dead bodies, but ended up thinking that the more interesting question is how belief works. It was becoming clearer and clearer that people's beliefs do not form a consistent or coherent body of understanding. The more you try to find a unifying structure that holds them all together, the more slippery and contradictory they seem to get. It turns out that holding incompatible beliefs at the same time is easier than getting your head properly straight. Some wrinkles never seem to disappear, and attempting to iron them only puts more creases in.

During the autumn and winter of 2013, when Mark felt freezing cold all the time, he used to sit in his orange armchair, wearing four or five layers, staring into space, his face blank. Or, more often, he would go and lie in bed, trying to keep warm under the duvet, listening to the radio. He was bad-tempered and depressed. Much of the time, he was silent, and would respond minimally or not at all to our questions or conversation. Diane, my closest friend in Melton, called round less frequently, and eventually stopped coming altogether rather than face another icy blast of disdain. I began to make excuses to the few remaining visitors to our house because Mark was so unfriendly, and I felt embarrassed. In retrospect, I think it was probably his illness that caused both his feeling of being cold and his depression at that time. So, he carried on, sitting in his chair, sucking the joy out of the house, indifferent to all attempts to comfort or cajole. Rachel, a teenager by now, retreated to her bedroom. All the boys and I could do was endure, make him cups of tea, bring him blankets for the cold, and focus on trying to insulate ourselves from his bone-chilling misery.

As part of my strategy to get us out of the house as much as possible, I spent half my waking life up at Burrough Hill, walking the Iron Age ramparts, while the boys, bundled up against the cold, made dens in the gorse or collected fossils. When darkness or the weather or flat refusals to go on another walk kept the kids inside, I escaped on my own, striding along Sandy Lane and out between the fields, looking for lapwings or hares. Drunk on fear and anger, I easily and regularly lurched off the edge of emotional equilibrium into tears or petulance. When I saw lapwings over the old airfield, tumbling out of the sky, they seemed in some way totemic, portentous. They made me happy. I found them profoundly moving, and myself rather ridiculous and sappy for responding that way. I seem to be especially susceptible to the charisma of these birds. I love their exuberant, twisting, inelegant flight, their big, square, flappy wings. I love the cleverness of them; they are supposed to feign injury to lure predators away from their chicks in their nests on the ground, though I have never witnessed this behaviour. People used to think that lapwings could turn into hares, and that baby hares – leverets – hatched from lapwing eggs. Some people have suggested that this is the origin of the Easter bunny myth. Hares make their nests, called forms, in shallow scrapes in the ground, in exactly the sort of locations lapwings prefer for their own nests. Sometimes, apparently, a pair of lapwings will even use an abandoned hare's form to lay their own eggs, and so the myth of the egg-laying hare – or, later, bunny – was born. Maybe. In any case, there is something joyful about these protective parents, these ungainly, headlong aerobats.

Well, here is something I would not admit to anyone at the time. I am a rational person, a humanist, not religious, not even 'spiritual'. When friends talk about the pull of religious faith, or their belief in a higher power, I feel the long miles of incomprehension stretching out between us. I would tell anyone that the world and the people, creatures, plants and things in it are enough to fill my life and give it meaning, without any supernatural varnish. Yet, during this period, I became secretly obsessed with signs, portents, omens. This is quite at odds with my academic self, and even with my usual personality, which is rational, critical, logical. I took each encounter with a lapwing, like each sighting of the first nail-paring of a new moon, as a moment of optimism, an assurance of things working out. I could have told you on any day exactly what phase of the moon we were at. I still can: a legacy of that time of my life, I suppose. I wished. I made my own half-mad spells. Adam, when he was about ten, told me that, if he glanced up at his digital clock and the time was symmetrical, he got a wish and it came true. It had to be visually symmetrical, not palindromic – so 22.55 counts, 13.31 doesn't. Henceforth, I followed his rules devoutly. Eleven minutes past eleven: time for a wish. I was embarrassed by my secret preoccupation with reading entrails. I have not mentioned this to my civilian friends, but my comrades in bereavement might understand. I heard a young widower on the radio – a doctor, so presumably a man of generally scientific and logical beliefs – confess his own surprisingly irrational adherence to a set of superstitious and compulsive beliefs during his wife's final illness; and it was no accident that the brilliant Joan Didion called her memoir of a shocking double bereavement *The Year of Magical Thinking*.

Some of my irrational practices at this time conformed to widely recognized folk beliefs, such as the habit I developed of saluting magpies. Because I did not want anyone else to know how insecure my grip on reality had become, if I was in company when I saw a magpie, I perfected a technique of lifting my hand to my forehead as if to scratch it, then sneaking in a quick salute before nonchalantly adjusting my hair or smoothing my eyebrow. Other irrational beliefs, however, came from my own mind, personal bargains with the cosmos allowing me to read auguries in whatever phenomena I chose. I developed obsessions not only with the new moon and lapwings, but also with a lucky bra, saved for important days like Mark's medical appointments, and I convinced myself of the auspicious properties of having muesli for breakfast. I attributed special significance to sundogs, those bright spots in the sky either side of a low sun, with their rainbow cloud around them, like oily puddles brilliantly translated into light.

Given that, through all of this, I still did not, and do not, believe in God, and did not at any time feel moved to prayer, when I made my wishes, who was I talking to? I could not tell you. I cannot justify or explain this craziness, except that it is to do with a lack of, not control, but of predictability. It was of a piece with my incessant making of plans – twelve-month plans, five-year plans, next-summer plans – each one modelling a different set of circumstances. If, then – a desperate attempt to organize a random and unpredictable world into a shape I could handle.

In the winter of 2014, I became obsessed with the hazel tree in front of the kitchen window. I told myself that, when it lost all its leaves, I would know what was going to happen. There were many weeks when it only had a very small number of leaves left, then only two, and then, inevitably, those two leaves also fell – but, disappointingly, still I knew no more. I set another deadline, and another, each one marking a point when there would be some clarity. Some of them were sensible: when we get Mark's next set of test results, or he has his next consultant appointment, we will get a prognosis, a timescale. Some were ridiculous: by the time of the next new moon; when we finish this jar of marmalade. None of them delivered the result I wanted.

It does not take a degree in psychology to see why I started grabbing at superstitions and magical thinking of my own making. I was waiting obsessively for news, for a prediction of what would come next, for progress one way or the other, for something to happen. And this desire to know was exacerbated by my own helplessness, by my inability to make things better, by not even knowing if I could or should be trying to make things better. I started looking for correlations. When anything good happened, what had led up to it? If I were to repeat those same steps, might I get a similar reward? So, if I put on the same bra I was wearing when we were told that Mark did not have a brain tumour, and ate the same breakfast, maybe there would be more encouraging news? I am an academic and I absolutely know that this is not how the world works. It is hard to explain the double-think that goes on with this kind of belief. I recognized in myself exactly the same capacity for holding incompatible beliefs that I had noted in the people of the seventeenth century. I knew it was rubbish, based on nothing, but I put the lucky bra on anyway.

It reminded me of the time when I was reading lots of folklore for an academic book I was working on. As part of this research, I read a work by the Scottish clergyman Robert Kirk, *The Secret Commonwealth* – the inspiration, in some ways, for Philip Pullman's novel of the same name. Based on stories he collected in the early 1690s, the book is, more or less, a natural history of fairies. Kirk believed unquestioningly in the existence of fairies. He would no more doubt their existence than he would doubt that there were blackbirds or squirrels. Kirk was a devout Christian, the first man to translate the Bible into Gaelic, so his challenge was to find how fairies fitted into the Christian universe. He argued that they were not evil spirits or creatures of darkness, but an intermediate order between men and angels. They had transparent bodies he described as being either congealed air or condensed cloud, but could be seen by those who looked for them. He described the places one was most likely to encounter them, which was near the mounds they inhabited, in or next to churchyards, and the best time of day to encounter fairies, which was evening. The book combines abstruse theology with something like a spotter's handbook. Even a fairly brief immersion in Kirk's work, though, changed the way I experienced the world. At that time, I liked to break up my writing and research days with a walk or a run, from our house on the edge of Melton Mowbray, down Sandy Lane to where it turns into an unsealed track and then just a path through the fields. I found that, in the few days after reading *The Secret Commonwealth*, I was keeping an eye out, when I got to the quiet places, for fairies, in the sort of terrain they liked. I delayed my jaunts so that I would be out at twilight, their most active time. Of course, I do not believe in fairies. But Kirk's conviction was so compelling. He lived in a world of unseen and half-seen beings, as well as the beasts of farm and wood that we all recognize, and I wanted to live there too.

15

FELO DE SE

I remember when Mark first started thinking that his illness might not be curable. We were in the kitchen, in Melton. I was just back from Tesco, and there were bags of groceries on the floor and on the kitchen table. Mark picked up a claw of celery and took it over to the fridge. Then, hidden by the open fridge door, he asked me, 'At what point do you think you take matters into your own hands?'

I have a book on parenting teenagers that advocates a technique they call side-by-side listening. Noting that it can be hard for a child to open up when sitting opposite a parent in a quiet space, when eye contact is inevitable, for important conversations with a teenage child, the book advises choosing a moment when you can avoid one another's eyes, taking some of the heat out of a potentially dangerous exchange. Driving a car at night, for example, is ideal. The driver has to focus on the road, and the passenger is free to look or not look. I think Mark was doing something similar in raising this issue when we both had our heads in cupboards and fridges, moving round the room, carrying out a task that did not require great concentration, but did mean that we were not looking at each other. How to answer? I knew exactly what he was talking about, and I took the coward's way out.

'I suppose, if one felt there were no hope of improvement, or if suffering was so terrible that it would be better to feel nothing at all, ever again. If a person was sure that there was no hope, or if the hope was so tiny and distant they just couldn't hold on for it, maybe then.' A person! What a cop-out.

Mark carried on, taking the wrapper off a multipack of yoghurts so they could all squash into our overstuffed family-of-five fridge.

'How do you know when you've reached that point, do you think?'

'I don't know. Doctors tell you, maybe? Or maybe they don't. Maybe you'd know, if you got there.'

We had silently made a pact to have this conversation as an impersonal one.

'It would be hard for your friends and family, though,' I observed, neutrally, as I added a couple of tubes of toothpaste to the pile of things to go upstairs. 'If they knew about your plan and didn't stop you – well, how would that be? Could you stand by, while somebody you love dies, if you could prevent it? How would you live with yourself afterwards?'

'But if you loved a person and saw that, for them, every morning that they woke up and knew they hadn't died in the night was a disappointment. If they wanted to be able to make it all stop, wouldn't you want that for them too?'

I wish I could slap this cautious, fearful me, make her take this chance to talk properly, but the stakes were too high, and I was too blindsided, too unprepared. Why did I not say something like, 'Whatever comes, you won't be on your own. Tell me what you are thinking, and I will try to support you in whatever ways you want, if I am able to'? Or, even better, why did I not just hug him? But instead I carried on, addressing my life partner as if he were a seminar.

'I think, if I were in that situation, I'd maybe want my pain to end,' I said, 'but I'm not sure I could actually do it. I mean, swallow those tablets or jump off that bridge or whatever. I think I'd be too scared.' I was talking too fast and too brightly, tearing the grocery receipt into unnecessarily small pieces and sprinkling them into the recycling. 'Do you really think you could? How would you do it? Who would find your body?'

Mark made a noncommittal noise. 'Yeah. I don't know.' A longer pause. 'Don't we already have about three boxes of Shreddies?'

In Jojo Moyes's novel *Me Before You*, the main character, Will, paraplegic after an accident and living a life he finds intolerable, decides to end his life by travelling to a euthanasia clinic in Switzerland. His girlfriend and carer, Lou, is appalled, and tries everything she can think of to dissuade him, but he is adamant, and she decides in the end to accompany him, reluctantly, on his journey to the clinic, and to be with him when he dies. Afterwards, she encounters hostility and censure from those around her. Even her mother treats her like a murderer. Lou's response to her boyfriend's situation was completely different from how I responded to Mark's desire for his life to be over, and none of those who knew us held this desire or Mark's eventual actions against either of us, as far as I am aware. During that first conversation, I felt a sinking fear for Mark, and a stifling anxiety about how I ought to respond and whether I would be up to scratch, whatever 'scratch' was, in this case. But, from the start, I could see how not existing at all might be preferable to existing in worsening pain and decreasing capacity. When life is just breathing, what kind of life is that? And, even if there are moments of engagement, moments of pleasure, is that enough if you cannot walk, talk, do what you want to do, make plans and carry them out?

The same afternoon that Mark had raised the subject, I took the boys on a visit to see my friend Lin, a former colleague who lived in the neighbouring village of Long Clawson, the same person who did the research on loom weights and women in the ancient Greek world. We had been enticed over by the promise that the boys could help Lin's husband, Hamish, make a bonfire in their huge vegetable garden – plus, it was a chance to get them out of the gloom of our house. Hamish is a wiry man, then in his mid-sixties, with a mop of grey hair and a bushy beard. I have rarely seen him dressed for anything other than the garden, with loose old trousers tucked into wellies, and a baggy jumper with holes in the elbows. Lin is a similar age to her husband, her long grey hair usually tied up in a precarious bun, which frequently droops away from her head and requires constant refastening. She is tall, pipe-cleaner thin and dresses like a bohemian teenager from the 1980s. As Hamish and the boys dragged dead branches up from the far hedge, Lin and I sat on mismatched chairs by the big dresser in her kitchen. There was a fistful of untrimmed radishes by the sink, some dough rising in a tea-towel-draped bowl next to the Rayburn. Lin made tea for us and pushed a pile of papers towards the middle of the table to make room for our mugs. Everything shifted a little, like the coins in a penny-falls arcade machine. Lin and Hamish are about fifteen years older than me, and had the kind of life Mark and I hoped to have in the future: their children were happy and established in their adult lives; their time was divided between academic work, cooking, gardening and their numerous hobbies. They made time for theatre and concerts, had a book habit that no twelve-step programme could touch, involved themselves in village life and leaped fearlessly into new interests and causes. But that day I was thinking that our future could be quite different. What if Mark did not get better? What if, instead, he got sicker? What if gardening, or salami-making, or editing, politics, teaching – what if all those things became impossible for him? And, ignobly, I was wondering what that would mean for me. What would it entail to be a carer? Where would our money come from? Would I be able to carry on working, and could I earn enough on my own to take care of a house, three children and a disabled partner at the same time? Or what if I would be shaping a future alone, as a widow? Would I cope? And, if not, what was the alternative? I told Lin what Mark had said, and she did not look shocked at all. I think there are many, many people for whom the decision to end one's own life, when that life no longer gives you pleasure, and where there is little or no hope of that changing, makes total sense.

The annual Suicide Awareness Day is a busy time on Facebook. Friends who have not been bereaved by suicide share inspirational posters about the importance of talking and listening, but in the Bereaved By Suicide closed Facebook group to which I belong, none of the posts are of that nature. Many people put up simple memorials – photos of husbands and wives who have died by their own hand. But some are angrier. Suicide awareness is not distinguished, in most people's minds, from suicide prevention, and social media is bulging with articles, information posts and slogans that emphasize the responsibility of people close to at-risk individuals to recognize the warning signs and take preventative action. Many of those affected feel that this sort of advice implicitly blames the bereaved for failing to prevent a suicide. After all, if suicide can be prevented by recognizing the signs and seeking help, you would have to be stupid, wicked or psychopathic not to step in and save a life when you have the chance. But many of the grim members of the Bereaved by Suicide club are people who struggled for years to support somebody with mental or physical health issues, at great cost to their own happiness and that of their families. They *did* recognize the signs, they tried to get help, they were on constant alert, they found it hard or impossible to access professional help, or their spouse was unwilling to cooperate. As Lin pointed out to me that day, 'If somebody really wants to end their life, there is not much you can do to stop them.' The effort of trying to prevent a suicide, sometimes for years or over the course of multiple attempts, means being permanently on Code Red, replaying everything they said for clues or warning signs, minding your own words and deeds lest an unconsidered comment or misinterpreted decision sends your husband running to the garage to fit a hosepipe to the exhaust of his car. It means sickening anxiety whenever you leave the house; it means that your other responsibilities – to parents, friends, children, employers, colleagues – are displaced and you are always falling short. Your own well-being is removed entirely from the picture. Suicide cannot always be prevented.

And, in my view, suicide should not always be prevented. I do see that a life ended by a depression that could have been a temporary blip, or because of a situation that could change – debt or unemployment, say – is always a tragedy for the individual who dies and for the people who loved them. As Robin Williams said, suicide is a permanent solution to a temporary problem. But suicide as an alternative to unending suffering is surely a different matter. Williams's own suicide, some years later, was not the result of a depression from which he might recover, but followed worsening neurological symptoms, which were discovered, at his autopsy, to stem from Lewy body dementia.

'Going to Switzerland' is not a straightforward alternative to suffering. Neither euthanasia nor assisted dying is legal in any part of the UK, so, if you want to end your life, but are not physically capable of taking the active steps required, your options are limited. At the time of writing, physician-assisted suicide is legal in Belgium, Luxembourg, the Netherlands, Switzerland, Colombia, Canada, New Zealand and parts of Australia and the USA. To use the service provided by the Swiss Dignitas clinic usually takes at least three months from making first contact with the organization. It involves mandatory counselling, and people are only accepted for assisted dying after a full exploration of alternative therapies that might address their suffering. Dignitas will not arrange for an assisted death – 'accompanied suicide' is the term they use – unless there is confirmed medical evidence of 'medically-diagnosed hopeless or incurable illnesses, unbearable pain or unendurable disabilities'. Without a diagnosis, it is not at all certain that Mark would have been successful in applying to Dignitas.

For people living in Britain, using Dignitas means a drawn-out set of procedures and a very expensive trip abroad. A recent report estimated the cost, for a British person, of dying through Dignitas at about £10,000 to £16,000, putting such an option beyond the reach of most seriously ill people in this country. To end your life at the Dignitas clinic, you also need to be well enough to travel to Switzerland.

Dignitas does offer, though, for those who have made up their minds, who do not think that any other alternative would suit their needs, a painless and certain way of dying, under proper supervision, at a time of the person's choosing and, crucially, with a chance to say goodbye to those close to them, and they do not have to die alone. The Dignitas website says:

DIGNITAS also advises the member that, whenever possible, it is extremely important to inform family and friends about the planned event as early as possible. This gives them the opportunity to be with the member until the very last moment.

... Preparation for and, most importantly, participating in the event itself are effective in helping all those who are left behind after the loss of a relative or friend to work through the loss and mourning process more easily. Someone who goes through the process can rightly feel that, by accompanying their loved one and performing a sacrificial service of love, they have shown their loyalty right to the end and enabled everyone involved to bid farewell to one another in peace.

Interestingly, only around 70 per cent of those who get a preliminary green light for an accompanied suicide from Dignitas ever take their attempt any further. Simply knowing that the option to end their suffering is there, should they need it, can be enough of a comfort to enable a person to go on with their life until it ends naturally. A study of physician-assisted suicide in the Netherlands showed a similar result. Dutch law allows people to obtain a fatal dose of a suicide drug if they can demonstrate to a doctor that their suffering is unbearable and they have no prospect of recovery. Patients must show that they are firm and settled in their wish to die by repeating their request. Similarly, in the ten states of the USA that allow voluntary euthanasia, the patient has to ask for it twice, with a fifteen-day interval between, and then wait another two days before the medication can be dispensed. Even at that point, only two thirds of the people who are prescribed the lethal drugs ever take them. Maybe this is too trivial an analogy, but, the first time I gave birth, I wanted to be in a hospital so that, if the pain proved too much, I would be able to get an epidural anaesthetic. In the event, I did not ask for any pain relief stronger than gas and air – for that or for any subsequent labour. But, if I had been anxious about whether I would be required to endure more pain than I could bear, I might have been too frightened to give birth as naturally as I wanted, or to experience the remarkable thing as fully. Knowing there was an option made not taking the option possible.

As I write this, New Zealand has just announced the results of a referendum on whether to legalize assisted dying. There, the proposed legislation specifies that, to be considered for medical assistance to end your life, you have to be terminally ill and with a life expectancy of no more than six months. Assisted dying is to be reserved for those who are dying anyway. It will only hasten the inevitable – although, strictly speaking, I suppose that is what any form of suicide does. None of us is immortal. There are similar requirements to be terminally ill in those parts of the USA, Canada and Australia that have assisted-dying legislation. Elsewhere, it is enough to be suffering unbearably and without prospect of significant improvement – though, in Belgium, a delay of one month is required in cases where the patient is not terminally ill. I am somewhat confused by the requirement of limited life expectancy. Why should it be possible to avoid a short period of unbearable suffering, but not a longer one? Still, it is better than nothing. The New Zealand referendum has passed in favour of legalizing assisted dying. This is a good thing and a step in the right direction. My Kiwi friend, Richard, the computer scientist who introduced me to QALYs, told me that he was surprised to hear objections to the proposed reform, even from some of his generally liberal friends. Those objections were on the basis that standards of palliative care in the country needed to be improved first, so that nobody felt forced into suicide because of the lack of a good alternative. At first, this made some sense to me, but, on reflection, it only muddies the waters. It is quite obvious that palliative care should be excellent and available easily and immediately to everybody who can benefit from it, but this is a separate issue. Whatever palliative-care doctors say, it is not always possible to remove pain entirely, or not without removing from the dying person almost all awareness of their surroundings, to the point where it is impossible to imagine that being alive means anything more than continuing to breathe. Moreover, there are other agonies than physical pain, and no amount of morphine can bring vivid purpose, contentment or pleasure to a life from which it has entirely drained away.

From time to time, somebody will raise the question of assisted dying or voluntary euthanasia in the British Parliament. In 2019, my local MP Nick Boles introduced a debate on the subject, though it was just a discussion and not intended itself to change the law. Sheffield MP Paul Blomfield made a personal, powerful and visibly emotional contribution, telling the story of his own father's death. Shortly after receiving a diagnosis of inoperable lung cancer, his father had written notes, left small piles of money to settle outstanding debts, then had taken an overdose and gone into the garage at his house, closing the door behind him. He fixed a hosepipe to the car exhaust, turned on the ignition, and died there, alone, in a fume-filled garage. Because he wanted to avoid making anyone else complicit, he did not share this decision in advance with his partner or his family. If they had known of his plan and still failed to prevent it, those closest to him would have been liable to prosecution and even imprisonment under British law; it was because of this that Paul Blomfield's father died a lonely death. For some people, because of their religious beliefs, what Blomfield's father did was wrong. I do not share those beliefs, but absolutely respect people's right to follow their own creed around this issue. What we should not respect, however, is anyone's right to make a decision for somebody else on the basis of unevidenced and unshared spiritual beliefs.

In his speech to Parliament, Blomfield regrets especially that his father died sooner than he might have done otherwise, because he did not want to risk leaving it until it was too late, until he was unable to organize and carry out his own death. You can see this speech on YouTube. Blomfield's voice is breaking as he tells this story, and the normally hardboiled MPs sitting around him reach out instinctively to touch his hand or squeeze his shoulder. It is a moving moment. Most of us respond instantly and empathetically to another person's grief, but Blomfield's grief was more complicated than most adults experience at the death of a parent, because of the cold and derelict nature of the end of his father's life. Nobody should have to choke alone in a garage filled with carbon monoxide. Death is inevitable, but the way we shape it is up to us. Everyone should be able to die at a time of their own choosing, with their friends and family around them. If they elect to end their lives deliberately, they should be able to discuss this enormous decision with those closest to them. They should be able to say goodbye.

Mark's death came sooner than he might have wanted, because he was scared, as he said in his note, of being unable to carry it out by himself if he left it too late. Maybe he would have chosen to die at that time, anyway. His existence was not bringing him much pleasure, and there was no improvement to look forward to. But, whenever he might have wanted to end his life, I cannot believe he wanted to die alone, without saying goodbye to his family. I think how casually we said goodbye to him when we left for Ben's that Friday night. I was checking he had what he needed, and that the phone and his drink were in easy reach. Then a quick goodbye – did I kiss him on the cheek? I cannot even remember – and we were gone, distracted by escape and sunshine. What would he have said to me, if he could? And he must have known, through all the faffing with his tray and his bedside lamp as we prepared to set off that day, that this was our last parting, that he would never see me or his boys again. Did he know a few weeks earlier that it would be the last time he saw Rachel, when she went back to university? Or, on his sister's final visit, that it was the last occasion they would ever be together? How did he manage not to grip onto them when they leaned in for a goodbye kiss? How did he mange not to sob, and look so hard into their faces that, if looking and loving alone could accomplish it, he would have seared himself into their skin?

The one thing everyone knows about suicides in the past is that they had to be buried at a crossroads with a stake through their bodies. Like many things that everyone knows, this turns out to be wrong – or, at least, not quite so simple. Until the nineteenth century, the law specified that suicides should be buried in the road, though not specifically at a crossroads. But, even when taking one's own life was strictly forbidden by Church and state, the burial laws that excluded suicides from the burial grounds of their kin were frequently circumvented. By the eighteenth century, suicides were rarely convicted of a felo de se, a crime against the self, especially if they were respectable and familiar members of the community. Instead, a verdict of not guilty because of a disturbance of the mind allowed their families to inherit any property, and their bodies to be buried in the churchyard.

Indeed, a combination of surviving coffin plates with legible names and dates, osteological analysis and the discovery of additional documentary evidence allowed two London burials to be identified as suicides, despite their mortuary treatment being indistinguishable from other burials of their time, tucked into the high-status crypts of their parish churches, at the heart of their communities. The two nineteenth-century burials, one from St Bride's Church and the other from Christ Church Spitalfields, had suspicious bullet wounds to the head that are typical of suicide by shooting. One had a bullet hole in the skull, the other had been shot in the mouth. Because their coffin plates still had legible names on them, the excavators were able to trace the historical records of their deaths, and found that the coroner in both cases had judged the men to have died at their own hands, but to be innocent of the crime of suicide by reason of insanity.

Suicide has not been illegal for a long time. Yet failing to prevent somebody else doing this entirely legal thing is still popularly and even judicially regarded as potentially criminal. In 2005, journalist Jill Anderson was prosecuted at Leeds Crown court for failing to prevent her husband Paul's suicide at their rural home two years earlier. Paul was suffering from chronic fatigue syndrome, which caused him deep and unrelieved exhaustion, as well as physical pain. He had been ill for nearly the whole period of the couple's nine-year marriage and, by the time of his death, was largely bedridden. Their business suffered and they became bankrupt. Three times, he had tried to kill himself, and each time Jill had got him to hospital and his life was saved. Although she recognized his sincere wish to be free of his pain, she could not bear, she said, to lose the man who 'made life magical'. On the final occasion, in 2003, she arrived home from a shopping trip to find Paul on the verge of losing consciousness. He told her that he had taken enough pills to finish things, and fell asleep. This time, Jill did not call an ambulance.

'I felt defeated,' she said. 'I had to accept that he didn't want to go on. I didn't want to see him pumped full of drugs again, forced to stay alive when he didn't want to be.'

Instead, she lay down next to him and stayed by him until he died, at around 9.30 the following morning. At eleven o'clock, she called their doctor. Jill's great grief at the loss of her husband was tempered by a 'strange euphoria' that she had been able to have some peaceful, pain-free time with him as he died. Two weeks later, however, the police came to her house to arrest her for manslaughter and assisting suicide. The latter charge was dropped, because there was no evidence that she had procured or administered the fatal drugs, but the manslaughter charge was not so easily dismissed. Despite her lawyer's belief that it would never make it as far as an actual trial, she was pursued to the high court. After a public and very upsetting trial, Jill was eventually found innocent, in 2005, but only after two years of being treated as a criminal. She had to surrender her passport and make weekly reports to the police station. The trial combed through Paul's life, the lack of a terminal diagnosis, and Jill's apparent acceptance of his suicide. The prosecution returned again and again to her delay in calling the doctor. Paul's family, though estranged from him, publicly blamed Jill for his death. Paul's sister told the press, 'His death was unnecessary. The one person to whom he entrusted his care let him down. By any standards of human behaviour, we believe Jill's actions in failing to summon medical assistance were morally unforgivable.'

Jill's grief was greatly compounded by efforts to make her feel guilty, and the isolation and stress of a police investigation and criminal proceedings. What should have been the end of the nightmare became the start of another one.

Mark did not want that to happen to me, but he paid the price. My comfort is that he chose his own end, and he was rational when he made that choice. Unlike most suicides, he was not mentally ill. No voices plagued him, no senseless despair swamped him. So maybe, I hope, he embraced the feeling, in those last minutes, of life seeping out, of the slow eclipse of consciousness.

Pentobarbital is a painless barbiturate and, if taken at a high enough dose, and not vomited up, invariably effective. The search history on his computer showed he had done quite a bit of research into the surest and kindest way to end his life. I have no doubt that Mark wanted it to work. Next to his letters for us, he left a request that nobody try to revive him, should he still be alive when discovered. This was no cry for help. At the moment he took the drug (pills? A powder? A solution? I do not know what form it was in, except that he swallowed it), he wanted to die. Did he regret it in those moments between swallowing and dropping into darkness? I read once that somebody had tried to interview all the people who jumped off the Golden Gate Bridge and survived. All of them said that their last emotion, as they were dropping through the air, was regret. They realized, too late, that all the problems in their lives could be resolved, except that they had just jumped off the Golden Gate Bridge. Did Mark have a Golden Gate Bridge moment? Unlike those jumpers, though, he was not an otherwise healthy man who was suffering from depression. Death was coming for him anyway, and the chance of his problems being resolved, or his remaining life bringing much joy, was microscopic.

And yet, Mark did not have a terminal diagnosis. 'Going to Switzerland' was not an option for him.

The very day I found Mark's body, my brother-in-law, Jon, a doctor, told me he thought Mark would probably not have lived much longer anyway. Jon is an anaesthetist, specializing in intensive care. He is accustomed to seeing patients in the most serious states, and he deals with death every day. He has considerable experience of progressive neurological disease in general. After thirty years of that, he has a good sense of how a disease is progressing. Would Mark have waited for a natural death, if he had been sure it was coming soon? Or would he have decided to finish his pain and distress anyway? I do not know, but I wish his doctors had been able at least to make space to talk about his death, and that we had not all colluded in the story that we wanted Mark to stay alive as long as possible, no matter what the circumstances. Instead, there was no room for Mark to say he had now had enough, or for me to confess that I struggled with the idea of indefinitely postponing the rest of our lives to accommodate the biological support of a man who was so desperately unhappy. If we had known it was only for a few months, would we have been kinder to each other?

In 2016, the year Mark died, 5,965 deaths by suicide were registered in the United Kingdom, according to the Office for National Statistics. About three quarters of these were male. Men between forty and forty-four and men over ninety have particularly high rates. Overall, suicide rates have been declining for the last few years in the UK as a whole, though the number of suicide deaths in Scotland was a little higher in 2016 than the previous year. The most popular method of ending your own life in 2016 was suffocation, strangling or hanging, which are all grouped together in the statistics. The second most popular method was poisoning, mostly drug overdose. The proportion dying from self-initiated drowning, fractures and falls remained low and fairly constant. A WHO report in 2008 found that methods varied by country according to what methods were most easily available. In the United States, many people kill themselves with guns. In Hong Kong, they jump off buildings. The same report also found that, worldwide, men were likely to choose abrupt and violent methods, such as shooting or jumping, and women were more likely to choose quieter ways out, like poisoning.

Suicide was not decriminalized in the UK until 1961, meaning that, until then, if you tried and failed to take your own life, you would have been liable to prosecution afterwards. But those bullet-punched skulls in London show that, even when strict Christian doctrine demanded the exclusion of suicides from burial in consecrated ground, priests, doctors and neighbours usually agreed that the suicide was mentally ill and therefore could not be considered guilty of the premeditated and mortal sin of despair. And yet a death by suicide was not, nor is it yet, quite the same as other deaths. The compassionate treatment of suicide, even when it was technically illegal, was enabled by the line of argument that the person had died by their own hand because the balance of their mind was temporarily disturbed. Because suicide was not generally seen as a rational act, the fact of having deliberately done it was evidence enough of an unbalanced mind. Suicides were necessarily mad, because why else would you? Mental illness explained and excused the ultimate act of despair, but left its own stigma around both the deceased and the bereaved.

Some relatives of suicides find their friends unwilling to mention the person who has died, to avoid drawing attention to the family's shame and so as not to embarrass those left. To be bereaved by suicide, in many people's minds, is a failure of the bereaved, too – a failure to prevent a death. When love is supposed to make the beloved happy, to improve their life, what does it say about you that your beloved was so miserable they would rather be dead? Did you make them miserable instead of glad? At the least, you, the bereaved, the abandoned, the left behind, were not worth staying around for. Such thoughts might not be expressed by the bereaved or by their friends, but they underlie some of the silence, and the swerves and veers of conversations pulled away from those treacherous edges.

16

CAPACOCHA

Oh, the things I've seen. Mostly in photographs, admittedly, but my research has brought me face to face with images that go beyond the extravagant gore of film and TV killing sprees. I have seen photographs of exposed bodies after the dogs have been at them, pictures of corpses desiccated, pickled and burned, and I know what a body looks like after 250 years in a lead-lined coffin. Researching the process of embalming was eye-opening. But the only time I have had to stop researching and do something else was not in response to revulsion, but to the emotional toll it was taking. I was reading about the Inca *capacocha*, ritual sacrifice of children. According to historical sources, only the most beautiful, physically perfect children were used in *capacocha* offerings. They were sent from all corners of the Inca empire to the capital city, Cuzco, where they would be looked after and trained for the roles they were to play. Some children stayed in Cuzco as slaves or religious figures, but, when a *capacocha* sacrifice was to be carried out, two children, a boy and a girl, were chosen to be sent out to each of the significant high locations where the sacrifice was to occur. They travelled in straight lines, sometimes for many weeks or months, until they reached the place of the sacrifice, and there, after being given alcohol or drugs, the children were killed and buried or entombed as offerings to the gods. The historical accounts of Spanish chroniclers are triangulated with archaeological evidence. Because the *capacocha* locations tended to be high, dry and cold, the mummified bodies of the child victims have often survived. What broke me, reading the sources, was the detail that children too young to feed themselves or walk the long journey from Cuzco would be carried and breastfed by their mothers. This, even more than looking at the faces of the dead children, eerily perfect in their preservation, their knees drawn up to their chins, was unendurable to contemplate. There is no hierarchy of loss, of course. Nobody can know what anyone else suffers. But the empathetic leap required to imagine how it would be to give up your own child to death was beyond me. I was reminded of thirty years ago, when I was first reading and thinking about how different the emotions of people in the past might be from our own. Did these Inca mothers think their children would have a better, happier future in the arms of the *apu*s? Did they feel honoured? Were their children the lucky ones? Or were they unable to challenge the power of the men, the ruling Inca and his court, the priests? Did they feel angry, guilty, or eternally broken? Everyone's grief is their own, and projecting my own feelings is often stupidly wide of the mark. But I do it all the time.

For the *capacocha* children, for their parents, was this a willing sacrifice? Were they doing a far, far better thing in order that their communities, their families might thrive, even without them? Were they assured, like Carton, of a far,

far better rest? What did they really believe? Did belief and doubt about what happens next jostle for primacy in their minds and hearts?

In her book *I Found My Tribe*, Ruth Fitzmaurice talks about envying people with cancer. Fitzmaurice, who writes about her experience of her husband's motor neurone disease, describes the contrast between the social treatment of people with cancer and those with neurological conditions. Most obviously, many cancers are curable; MND is not. Also, there are benefits to having a disease which people recognize. Everyone knows what cancer is. In 2014, there was a minor outcry in the media because the Pancreatic Cancer Association ran a campaign featuring people with pancreatic cancer saying that they wished they had breast cancer, or testicular cancer or prostate cancer instead. Their point was that breast cancer is comparatively well understood, responsive to treatment and, these days, very often curable, in contrast to pancreatic cancer, which has a bleak prognosis and an average survival rate from diagnosis of four to six months. In those circumstances, people with pancreatic cancer often expressed a desire for the better odds of one of those other common cancers. However, people with breast cancer, and the relatives of those who had died from any of these 'less serious' cancers, objected to an implied hierarchy of suffering; they pointed out that these cancers were still often fatal, and that a campaign to raise awareness of one type of cancer should not work by minimizing the suffering or risks attendant upon others. Nobody with breast cancer feels themselves fortunate to have received such a diagnosis. However, the Advertising Standards Authority did not uphold the complaints received about the campaign. They cited the very poor life expectancy for pancreatic cancer in comparison to breast or testicular cancer, and the much smaller charitable income raised for pancreatic cancer (£4.5 million in 2012 for pancreatic cancer, as opposed to £41 million for breast cancer, according to a 2014 report).

Similarly, Ruth Fitzmaurice felt that, in comparison to MND, cancer is predictable, with known and well-established protocols, a range of treatment options, well-funded research programmes and new drug trials. She stopped well short of saying that people with cancer are in any way lucky. But I could totally understand how she felt. In fact, I would have felt that, compared to Mark's situation, people with MND were in a more privileged position. Reading her words, I found myself thinking, in an admittedly petty way, At least you have a diagnosis. At least the doctors have some idea of what will happen and when. You have support associations and an army of carers and volunteers who know what to expect and what can be done for people with MND. We just had a wilderness of uncertainty.

I feel similarly when I read Marion Coutts's account of the death of her husband Tom from a brain tumour. I know how small-minded and misdirected this is: her husband died, the love of her life. And they had a very young child at the time. But I am struck throughout by all the support she has: the hospitals and care framework that mostly works well for them. His GP knows him; carers and therapists are all arranged for them. Most of all, they have a huge network of local friends who take him to his appointments. Marion is able to organize a rota – *a rota* – of people to take him to several weeks' worth of radiotherapy; their house is always full of visitors, or they go out, since Tom is more or less mobile until the very last few weeks. She talks, as many bereaved people do, of being buried beneath a landslide of meals and gifts during Tom's illness. In his last few days, in a hospice, their room was full of friends and relatives. I should feel heartbroken for all that she has been through, and all that she has lost, and I do, but I also feel envy and a touch of shame. We did not really have any local friends, and fewer still after we moved. Mark was not a very sociable person, anyway. Only the most tenacious relationships with the thickest-skinned friends had survived the long years of his silent depression. I wish there had been more of a network of support for me and the children. And I also wish, now, that I had been able to create for him a more stimulating world, like Marion Coutts did for Tom. I wish I had tried harder to get him out of the house with the wheelchair. Our house could hardly have been worse for a man with serious physical disabilities. Why did we not think of moving house again? Even renting somewhere. Sometimes, I cut flowers from the garden and brought them to his room: daffodils and bachelor's buttons in the spring. But I did not cover the walls of his bedroom in artworks by friends and family. I know I could have tried harder, could have done more. It was all just too difficult, and too tiring. I knew how much he was suffering, how unrewarding his life now had become. My compassion should have been all for him, yet I swaddled myself in my own self-pity and let the bitterness grow. Marion Coutts, like a new partner's glamourous ex, is a rebuke, a standard by which I will always fail, the innocent focus of my own envy and resentment because of what she had, and I did not, and because of what she did and I failed to do.

Those unattractive feelings of self-pity and envy did not get any better after Mark died. About three months after his death, I was in Wickes, buying some paint rollers and four bags of cut-price potting compost. I was on my own, of course. The compost bags weighed a ton, and I struggled to get them onto the flatbed trolley. I could push the trolley to the car, but lifting the heavy sacks into the boot brought me to the limit of my physical ability. All around me were middle-aged couples, older than me, going in pairs to buy a screwdriver and some gardening gloves. Eventually, I managed to get the bags into the car, though one of them ripped as I scraped it over the catch, and consequently there was compost all over the boot. I got into the driver's seat, closed the door and cried. This was not just a moment of tearfulness, such as I was prone to in the queue at the supermarket checkout, but proper full-on howls for being alone, and not really managing, and not having what all the women in the car park had: somebody to share the work. No. It was more specific than that. Though I knew I should not feel it, and despite my lifelong adherence to feminist principles, I felt the lack of a man, who would lift and carry things, and know how to fix things, and do DIY jobs. I wanted a man. Not, at that stage, for love or companionship, or even sex. I wanted him for putting bags of compost in the boot, fixing the shower, looking after the car, cutting the hedge, replacing the fire alarm. I was out of my depth and there was nobody to rescue me. I did not know what I was doing, I did not have the experience or skill or knowledge. Sometimes, I did not have even the physical strength or the height. And, despite all the belief in equality I have grown up with, and to which I subscribe, I did not at first have the confidence to attempt what my mother used to call Y-chromosome jobs. This was a low point.

I found that there were certain places, in my newly widowed state, that made me feel particularly alone and out of step with society. DIY stores were one, with their populations of what I assumed to be competent men who know what they were doing. Supermarkets were another, or rather supermarket checkouts. It was the couples that got to me: shopping together, sharing the packing. I felt stressed, harassed, almost tearful trying to get everything into bags quickly. I hated those oblivious couples standing waiting for me to finish. At the same time, I was envious. The lack of a partner when visiting friends or meeting people socially did not bother me – we were never that sort of couple – but being the sole parent at children's occasions upsets me to this day: school events, concerts, parents' evenings when I am the only person there who is interested in my child. To my eye, it seems that every other child has a phalanx of parents, grandparents and other relatives; mine just have me, memorizing the concert programme because I do not have anyone to talk to.

In the last years of Mark's life, I found unexpected sanctuary in my car. The cultural geographer Marc Augé talks about 'non-places', places of little or no geographical specificity, liminal, in-between places: airports, stations, motorway service stations. For me, my car became my non-place. Out of it, I belonged to the world. I knew that I had constant responsibilities: the moment I walked through my front door, I was immediately confronted with the needs of my children, my partner, the endless demands of the house and its management; in the office, it was emails and marking and deadlines and perpetual requests for references, reports, reviews. But, while I was in the car, I belonged to nobody. I could not be expected to do anything else. Sometimes, I would drive as slowly as I reasonably could, willing the traffic lights to turn red, so that I would be able to put off the arriving a little longer. Sometimes, I used to sit in the university car park, or in the drive at home, gathering the daily fortitude to unclip the seat belt, get out of the car, organize my face into an expression of cheery calm, and prepare to open the door and face whatever might be behind it.

For a long time, I was preparing for Mark's death, though we did not know that he was going to die. I read other people's experiences, though mostly they were about the shock of responding to a sudden death. I thought constantly about what might happen, though no doctors had talked about it with us, feeling disloyal if I gave voice to the big, catastrophic thing. Even to imagine the death of the monarch used to be considered treason, punishable by beheading. Now, I was that traitor. Rather than speak the treason in my mind, I found other things to say, dull things. My life was nothing if not dull. I longed for a 'clean' bereavement or, failing that, for the clarity of knowing for sure whether or not bereavement was imminent. But we were neither here nor there: not abruptly torn apart, nor expecting a death, not exactly. It was our own particular limbo. Our non-place.

And my feelings were out of step with what other people describe and with what those around us imagined me to be feeling. As my research into *capacocha* sacrifices had shown, people confronted with death and loss do not always respond the way you think they would – and, among those people, I include myself. I was silenced by shame because nobody else was saying anything like this, but, by the spring of 2016, I wanted an end to it, one way or another. A better Mark no longer seemed to be possible. I longed to have control over my life and my time again. I longed to make a different kind of life than the truly shitty one I currently had, and I could not see how that would be possible with Mark like this. We were not happy together, but could not be apart. Unless he could recover to a level where he could function without me, death seemed to be the only way this could end. At hospital appointments, I willed Dr Leite to give us the comforting clarity of hope or hopelessness, to stop what, a few years after the onset of symptoms, felt like stringing us along, although I know that was never her intention. Instead, she talked brightly about other treatments we might try, and sounded pleased to tell us all the conditions that Mark did not have: no sign of cancer! Negative for Creutzfeldt–Jackob disease! And all the areas where he was not declining: the muscle tone in his hands is still good! Great. She thought this was what we wanted to hear, that this was, all things considered, good news and a comfort.

17

ANTHROPOLOGIE DE TERRAIN

Taphonomy is the study of how living things die, decay and become buried or fossilized. The French anthropologist Henri Duday developed a taphonomic approach to the study of human remains that he called archaeothanatology, or *anthropologie de terrain,* anthropology of the ground. By meticulously and precisely recording the position of every bone and its spatial relationship to surrounding elements, *anthropologie de terrain* can reconstruct the exact sequence and conditions of a burial. By disentangling the patterns produced by decay from those produced by deliberate human action, we can pick out the practices that people used to control death and the dead. Duday and his students developed techniques to tell whether a burial is primary, i.e. in its original location, or secondary, i.e. it has been moved from its first place of interment, whether the ground was filled in around it or it lay originally in an empty space such as a coffin, even when there is no sign of the coffin now. The bones of a wrapped or tightly enclosed body will not collapse in the same way that an uncontained one will. Because the ligaments that hold bones in position decay in a predictable order, the degree of articulation in human remains tell us whether any disturbance happened soon after burial, when soft tissue had not yet decayed (as happened to those Christians whose buried bodies were dug up and dumped under a big, alien boat at Balladoole), or long after, when bones were quite separate (like the remains sorted by element and organized into patterns in the Paris catacombs). Sometimes, not as an archaeologist, but as a person who does not understand or cannot quite remember what has happened or how, I rely on material traces to help me reconstruct things that happened very recently. A parcel on the step tells me the post came. A note, a report, a text – all help me fill in gaps. My own everyday *anthropologie de terrain*.

Saturday, 7 May 2016, in the morning. I sat on the front step of the house, waiting for the ambulance. Should I call my brother and ask him to tell the boys, or should I wait till after the police have been, and Mark's body has been taken away? The weather was beautiful still. The cherry tree in front of the house was shedding blossom, and little twisters of pale pink drifted across the drive. The sun was warm on my face and arms. Maybe the incongruity of the perfect May morning with the momentous nature of what was happening contributed to a curious kind of detachment. I waited on the step: neither in the house, nor out of it. On a threshold in more than one way, a non-place. Rachel sent me a text to let me know she had passed her driving theory test. I did not reply. I did not cry. It was a strangely vivid interlude of quiet: the confetti swirl of the cherry blossom, the birdsong, the warmth, waiting. There were the familiar sounds of

Saturday morning. Somewhere across the railway, a road-breaker's drill vibrated, ringing like a school bell. From our house, near the town centre, you can often hear the keening of ambulance and police sirens. Now, I was waiting for one of them to grow louder, but the ambulance, when it came, had no lights or sirens.

The ambulance turned into our drive, and a police car immediately behind it. I did not move from the step while I heard doors open and close. Two paramedics appeared, carrying their heavy resuscitation equipment.

I looked up at them. 'You won't be needing that.'

WITNESS STATEMENT: 09/05/2016

I am a serving Police Officer with Lincolnshire Police. I make this statement in relation to an incident that I attended on Saturday 7 MAY 2016.

At 09.36 hours on Saturday 7 MAY 2016, I was deployed by Airwaves to attend a report of a sudden death. I arrived on scene at 09.46 hours that same day. As I arrived, Ambulance staff had just arrived and were on the scene. On arrival, the front door to the property was open and I entered the property. I spoke with a female who gave her name as SARAH TARLOW. SARAH told me that she was the wife of MARK PLUCIENNIK.

SARAH showed me to an upper-floor bedroom to the rear of the property where I could see a male lying in a hospital-style bed. The bed was in the middle of the room, with the head of the bed located to the left-hand side wall of the room, and the foot of the bed to the right-hand side wall.

SARAH identified the male as being her husband MARK. She informed me that she had been away for the evening and had returned home around 09.15–09.20 hours to find MARK had passed away. MARK was cold and rigid and his skin was grey and dull. Ambulance staff confirmed that MARK was deceased and that in their opinion he had died several hours before our attendance.

I went over to the bed and checked MARK for any injuries. MARK was lying on his back, and wearing a grey T-shirt with no bottoms. MARK had a yellow duvet covering him. I could see that MARK had a catheter as the bag was attached to the side of the bed and partially filled with urine.

To the right of the bed was a set of drawers, which had three drawers. The middle drawer was completely removed and was on the floor. Both top and bottom drawers were open and contained medication.

Also to the right-hand side of the bed was a bedside table with wheels which goes over the bed. It had a cylindrical plastic container on it, which had no label. The container was totally empty. Next to the plastic container was a note written on two pages of lined A4 paper, believed to have been written by MARK. The note had messages to his friends and family. At 10.25 hours that same day, I seized the note, and at 10.30 hours I seized the plastic container. The plastic container was placed into an Exhibit Bag and was later booked into the temporary property store at GRANTHAM Police Station.

To the left of the bed was a white cabinet and on top of the cabinet was an A4 printout containing information on the drug 'Pentobarbital.' MARK had mentioned in his note that he had taken this drug to end his life. At 10.35 hours that same day, I seized the printout.

SARAH explained that MARK was suffering with a Progressive Neurological Disorder which was not fully diagnosed but believed to be Encephalomyelitis. MARK was being cared for by the local Community Care Team and by his wife. She also told me that he had a poor standard of living in relation to being able to get out and do daily tasks.

SARAH assisted me in collecting all of MARK'S medication, some of which was in the bedroom drawers and the majority was in a lower kitchen cupboard. I seized the medication and booked it into the temporary property store at GRANTHAM Police Station for destruction.

The police officer steered me into the front room and sat me on the sofa. She wanted to make me a cup of tea, but I did not want tea. I was not crying then, and I felt quite rational. I had rehearsed in my mind how it would be when Mark died, and now it was really happening, pretty much exactly as I had imagined it might. In response to her questions, I described as best I could the events of the last twenty-four hours, and some of the context of the last few years. The paramedics came down and filled out their paperwork, not rushing now. PC Kelly went back upstairs to record the scene for her report. When she came down, she said that Mark's body could be taken away, and so, if I wanted to go and say goodbye, I should do so now.

Standing by his bed, I felt the grief pushing up behind

my face – grief and guilt, and, most of all, pity for everything he had been through, and for what it had come to.

'Oh, darling,' was all I could manage. And then, 'I'm sorry. I'm so, so sorry.'

I did not call my brother Ben until the undertakers had left. The police officer had not wanted to leave me on my own, and she'd seemed a little wrong-footed by me declining her offer to make me a cup of tea, or to call somebody to come and be with me, but finally she too went away. I knew I had to tell the children. Like a coward, I called the people Rachel was staying with and asked them to tell her. Then I phoned Ben, hoping they would not yet have left for their day out by the lake. They had not.

'Ben.'

'Oh, hi, Sarah.'

'Ben.'

'Yes. This is Ben.'

I paused. No good words.

'Mark's died.'

I told him, briefly, what had happened and asked him to tell Adam and Greg. I found out later that Ben had taken the boys into one room to break the news, while his wife Katy spoke to their own children in another. So I was spared having to find words to tell my daughter or my sons that Mark had died. Emotionally powerful moments – being told shocking news is the best example – are retained in the memory with particular clarity. That is why everyone remembers where they were when they heard that Princess Diana had died, or that two planes had flown into the World Trade Center. My friend Helen's husband died suddenly and unexpectedly while he was out riding his bike. Helen found out what had happened when a policeman came to the door. She still remembers going upstairs to tell their daughters the news, and thinking, I must get this right.

That is the thing with words. We model things in them like wet clay we never intend for firing. Words tend to solidify things, which can be frightening, and can sometimes make something out of nothing, or nothing out of something. I struggle with this, because I am so full of words. But, if I let them all out, all my words and feelings, you would be drowned in them. I did not know what to say about Mark and his death for a long time, because there seemed to be too much, and it was too ill-arranged. I was trying all the time to moderate the flow, to hold back my words, especially in front of the children. When this dam crumbles, I thought, there will be the mother of all floods.

I called my sister, Jo, and Mark's sister, Susan. Both Mark's parents were dead, so his sister and her son were his only family. Other friends and things could wait. I was not crying. I did not want tea. I went on sitting on the step, in the sun.

And now he is dead, I was thinking, what is this? How am I, now? I used to think I knew how it would feel, the death of a spouse. The desperate sickening pain of it. When my father died, that was grief, a grief that only takes from you, peels you away, leaves nothing in the middle. Grief that lies in wait in empty armchairs and unsolved crossword clues. It still, ten years on, ambushes me when I am weeding the garden or in the middle of a run, and I am suddenly, embarrassingly, sobbing by a hedge and I cannot get my breath. Grief is your life as it was before, but less. A diminishing. It is a stripping away, or a hollowing out, and it hurts. There is nothing pleasurable in it, but there is a kind of purity.

But this death was something different. It did not feel like grief, as I had experienced it for other relatives or friends over the years, though I did find myself rinsed, from time to time, by the tears that appeared on my face, apparently from nowhere. Mostly, I was dry-eyed and exhausted. For a couple of weeks, I did not fancy eating. I had a light-headed, dreamy, unreal feeling. I was not sleeping well, with Greg wriggling in next to me for comfort, and I woke early in the summer dawns, and wondered, What now?

18

GRIEF AND A HEADHUNTER'S RAGE

'There are no timely deaths,' said the rabbi at my uncle's funeral recently, 'though some are more accepted than others.' Mark died young for a man in Britain today, but he was old enough to have lived a substantial life. Not enough for anyone at his funeral to utter the words, 'a good innings', thank God, but he might have had much less. He was no *capacocha* sacrifice. There is no rule, though, that deaths hurt less if they are expected; people are not missed less because they are old. The right words, the right thoughts can help in bereavement, and it has been my job to find those for the non-religious funerals I take.

Three days before Mark died, I was officiating at a funeral in Grantham. I remember it well because the woman who had died, Joan Gilliver, had, unusually, wanted to meet me, in the final weeks of her life, to talk about the funeral and how she wanted to be remembered. She had enjoyed a good life, by anyone's standards: lots of overseas travel, a devoted husband, three healthy and successful children, and a full and adventurous retirement. As always, most of the ceremony was about Joan's life and character, but I also had to find words to reassure and comfort the bereaved, if that was possible.

'Nothing can compensate for the absence of Joan, and there is no silver lining to this cloud,' I told them. 'But we can hold on to the knowledge that, even when a bright and fierce fire like Joan's goes out, she has lit flames that survive. Joan survives in your hearts and memories. She survives in the lives that would be different, and worse, if she had not touched them. She survives in her children and grandchildren.

'Our task now is to return to our own lives, inspired by her zest and warmth, and to reach out to others and illuminate their lives where we can, as she lit up ours. Think of Joan on a spring morning when you're potting on the bedding plants; think of her when you're heading for a cool drink after an energetic game of tennis; think of her when you gather with friends and talk and laugh. Raise a glass to her then, but go on talking and laughing, because that, more than sombre silence or reverential gloom, is the spirit of Joan.'

I liked the words, at the time, but did not deeply feel their import until a few days later. Joan's funeral was on a Wednesday. I remember going straight from the crematorium to Halfords to collect the car from its service and pick up the bike I had ordered for Greg's birthday on Thursday. The following Saturday, Mark died, and very soon I came to appreciate how important it is to be given space not only to grieve, but also to smile and joke; to be given permission not only to feel sorrow, but also to feel hope and joy. My experience was not what I had expected the loss of a spouse to be like: I had imagined I would be crying constantly and overwhelmed by sorrow. I think many people have an expectation that this is how it will be. I remember thinking before Mark's funeral that I had to be the kind of widow other people needed me to be – to enable their own grief by offering mine as something with which they can empathize. A lightning rod of sorrow. I am not the only person to worry that I was not grieving right, that people would be shocked if they saw me smile or make plans for a future without him. As a funeral celebrant, my role is short and defined. I hope to be a comfort in the immediate aftermath of a death, but my relationship with the bereaved generally finishes once the funeral is over. In Joan's case, this was not quite true. When her widower, Bruce, sent me a thank-you email a few days later, he got my out-of-office message saying that my husband had died and I would therefore be slow to respond. He wrote me a very kind reply, even as he was immersed in his own grief. *Be strong*, he wrote. Four years later, I was able to say those same words at Bruce's own, small, lockdown funeral. Bruce and Joan's children have had their own experience of loss and, of course, everyone's grief is unique, but somehow, as an unintended consequence of trying to give comfort, I found some peace of my own in their stories. The best I can do as a celebrant is to honour the dead and to listen properly to the bereaved. I want them to know that tears are not shameful, but nor is laughter.

After Mark's death, in the space of one week, three of my friends urged me to go and see a counsellor. I knew that all three of them had benefitted from extended periods of counselling, although only one of them has been bereaved herself. All three had screwed-up childhoods and were still dealing with their batty parents; all three were carrying difficult family relationships into their adult lives. Although, by this point, my father had been dead for several years and my mother was lost to me because of her dementia, I was lucky to have had a good childhood, in a stable and kind family. So, to my knowledge, I had no childhood scars that needed addressing. Counselling, however, is ubiquitous in the places of bereavement, and indeed in the contemporary Western world more generally. I was resistant, for two reasons.

First, I had no idea who to approach. There were lists and registers online, each name accompanied by a smiling photograph and a paragraph about that person's areas of interest. How did anybody choose between them? They all offered the option of a trial chat to see if we were compatible, like an internet date, and I had been told to try a few people if necessary, until I found one I liked. Did that mean I would have to say, at the end of the trial session, 'No, you're not my type'? The thought was excruciating.

The larger issue was that I was not sure what exactly I wanted from counselling. I thought then, all things considered, I was doing OK. I was tired beyond belief, unsure of the future, could not be bothered with work, but these seemed rational and appropriate responses to my circumstances and recent history. I was not having panic attacks or constantly reliving the moment of finding him. My dreams were of Mark, but they were not nightmares. I was probably drinking more than I should be, but not at problem levels.

Probably. What should I ask for? What kind of help did I need from a counsellor?

I had reservations, because I had seen a counsellor before. Three years earlier, I'd had a couple of sessions through my workplace counselling service. Mark was ill and depressed, not getting on well with the children, who were, in turn, and partly for that reason, having troubles of their own. I was angry with Mark, uncertain of what to do for the best, feeling powerless to protect my children and unsure what Mark would need in the future, or what that future was going to be. I was aware that I was not putting anything like enough thought or energy into my job or my declining mother. The counsellor I saw was a tiny woman in office trousers and a billowy, floral top. She waited while I talked, asked some questions, and offered no advice or opinion, which I found frustrating. Towards the end of the second session, I found I was becoming tearful and angry while I was describing my predicament. The counsellor seemed pleased. This was progress, apparently. She asked me when I would know Mark's prognosis. As was often the case, I said we were waiting for the next scan or the next set of test results, and hoping they might give us some clarity. Perhaps it would be good to wait for those results before our next session, she thought. So I left, with no better sense of how to go on, no new insights into my own state of mind. I knew already that I was tearful and angry: that is why I had decided to try counselling. Rather than feeling helped by the experience, I got the impression that I had been a disappointing client for not having a clear-cut situation. If Mark had a terminal diagnosis, she could deliver the 'anticipatory grieving' protocol; if he recovered, we could be funnelled into normal relationship counselling. I was awkward, hard to contain, all knees and elbows, flailing and kicking in the dark.

I thought it likely that any counselling I got in the couple of years following Mark's death would be the same: the bereavement box. 'Grief work'. Another standard procedure that would not fit. I felt the distance between my response and those of other bereaved people I knew or read about. The cancer deaths, the traffic accidents, the sudden heart attacks. What was counselling going to do? What I wanted was practical help. I wanted somebody to take down the overgrown leylandii in the front garden and sort out the damp in the hall floor. I decided, instead of a counsellor, I would use the money to pay somebody to cut the grass for six months, and get a plasterer and a painter to redecorate the room that had been Mark's.

Mark was not offered counselling during his illness, although he was given two psychiatric assessments. On the first occasion, around the same time that I had seen the lady at work, Mark was referred to the local NHS mental-health service by the GP, when he finally, under pressure from me, consulted her about his depression. I have in front of me the self-assessment form he filled out before the consultation. He had to score how often in the last two weeks he had been bothered by various feelings or behaviours. I see that he scored himself at the highest level for 'feeling depressed, down or hopeless', 'feeling that you are a failure or have let yourself or your family down' and 'thoughts that you would be better off dead'. On the risk assessment, he answered yes to every stage of considering, planning and working out a method for killing himself, and wrote that only fear for the impact on the children was stopping him from doing it right then. I did not see either the form or the letter that followed the appointment, until after he had died.

He must have felt so alone in those last few weeks. Where I had the emotional support of friends like Sarah and Diane, who gave me space to talk about what was happening to us and how I felt, no comparable outlets were available to Mark. He had few friendships, and they were characteristically masculine in style: people to do stuff with, talk about the world, about politics or to joke with, but not people with whom he could talk about feelings, relationships, his own self. Maybe a counsellor or psychiatrist without a suicide-prevention brief might have been able to help. But we were different people, in that respect. Where I wanted to talk openly to pretty much everyone we knew about what was happening, he was private and protective. Towards the end, he did not want people who had respected him to witness what he had become. Two of the office staff who had worked for him when he was at the university called to see when it would be convenient for them to visit, but Mark would not let them come. He had only me as a confidante, and I had precisely none of the emotional distance or disinterest that would have made for a good listener. Also, of course, I was part of the problem.

Mark did not deliberately conceal his illness, but, because he rarely saw people face to face, and was naturally parsimonious with personal information, his death came as a shock to most people who had not seen him for a while. Some of them did not even know he had been ill, and only a few understood how ill he was. We had lived, like many people of our age and background, without putting down deep roots anywhere. Our friends were mostly at work, and since we commuted to work in another town, when he retired, those connections soon atrophied. Apart from the children and me, the only people to see Mark in those last months were his sister Susan, a couple of my friends, his ex-wife Hilary and our friends Simon and Pim. Other friends had seen him in the early part of his illness, when he was still walking, talking, giving the appearance of functioning normally. He never wanted anyone outside the family and his medical team to know how terrible he was feeling. The day after he died, I sent an email to about a dozen friends, giving the news and asking them to pass it on. That email, and the Facebook posts and the phone calls from friend to friend, must have crashed into their summer morning like a meteor, splintering the tranquillity with no warning, knocking them to the ground. The messages in those first days were mostly ones of bewilderment: 'I can't believe it', 'We didn't even know he was ill', 'I am too shocked to take it in properly', 'I can't believe it', 'I can't believe it', 'I can't believe it'. There they had all been, just strolling along on a summer day, and then a rustle of leaves, a breeze on their faces, and their friend, with his plans and his sharp mind and his young children, was suddenly dead in front of them. And he had been just fine, as far as they knew, and now he was dead.

Some of my friends are of the same mind as the counsellor I saw, that my anger is better out than in. They think that, if I do not let it out in a controlled way, slowly taking off the weight from the pressure cooker, with a tea towel round my hand, the boiling steam will explode from me in more damaging situations. But, for me, during the time of Mark's illness, pouring out rage and misery did nothing to reduce the amount inside. I was a magic porridge pot of anger, a volcano in constant eruption. After crying to one of my patient friends, all I wanted to do was cry some more. After I had lost my temper, the fury stayed in my blood, sometimes for weeks.

On my return from my first extended visit to Orkney, in the first year of my PhD, I told my supervisor that I no longer believed putting power relations at the centre of my study of changing funerary practices was going to be enough. What about feelings? And was it not excessively cynical to look at how a parent had buried their child and then interpret their memorial monument primarily as a bid for social status, a piece of mortuary one-upmanship? My supervisor suggested I take some time to think about what an archaeology of emotion, of loss might look like, and told me to read an essay by the cultural anthropologist Renato Rosaldo. Rosaldo had been doing ethnographic research among the Ilongot of the Philippines. At one time, the people Rosaldo wrote about had been famous headhunters. When he asked the older Ilongot men why they desired to take heads, they told him that rage, born of grief, drove them to do it. For a long time,

Rosaldo was unable to make sense of or elaborate on this concise statement, until a personal tragedy brought him a new, and unwanted, understanding. His wife, herself a promising cultural anthropologist, lost her footing on the edge of a precipice and fell to her death. Amid the shock and pain of this appalling rupture, Rosaldo was surprised to find how pervasive and clamorous was his own rage. His essay, 'Grief and a headhunter's rage', has since become a seminal essay in the anthropology of emotion, demonstrating the inadequacy of the traditional anthropological focus on ritual at the expense of bereavement, and criticizing the tendency of ethnographers to 'tidy away' the emotional aspects of the lives they documented.

I had not foreseen that anger would take up so much of my own emotional inventory in the misery of Mark's illness. I had expected to feel stress, grief, fear and depression, but, in those last weeks of Mark's life, rage was my most faithful and reliable companion. I was powered by wrath, always on the edge of an outburst. Mark was a big believer in anger. 'It is better than sadness,' he would say, 'better than self-doubt, than despair. Be angry,' he would urge. All his life, he was angry: with the government, with big business, with management, with the Americans or the Israelis, with capitalism, stupid people, football, dogs, rubbish, the state of the world. Most of the time, he had a good case. He expressed his anger freely, and wanted me to share it. If I did not, I learned quickly not to voice my own opinion, because it would inevitably lead to a row, which left him energized and me depleted.

By 2014, years of anger had fermented and gone bitter in my core, and much of it was focused, fairly or not, on Mark. I was at the same time frightened, full of pity for his pain, frustrated by our circumstances and his behaviour, furious at my own powerlessness. And I still loved him, I suppose. I was in the horror mansion, the Scooby-Doo house, in the dark, and I did not know what was in there with me, or where it might jump out from, or how to find my way back to the fresh air. I was too tired, too boiled down to be patient with all his opinions any more. I stopped looking for consensus and I let my anger show. To my shame, I also lost my temper easily with the children. I would come into a house where they had failed to clear away their breakfast things, or one of them would be complaining about something trivial, and I would slap them with my words, working myself up like a toddler in a tantrum, till I could feel my own heart beating fast, my teeth pressed together. At my worst, I would literally tear my hair out, grabbing great fistfuls and pulling at my scalp. When I could, I learned to walk away at this point, striding out of the house, breathing hard, channelling the adrenaline of my fury into physical movement, until my mind subsided into regret for my outburst. Then, I would slink back, apologize, get on with trying to be nice, pushing back all the stuffing that had come flubbing out of my worn seams, tacking together enough of a self to go on.

I wish I had been more patient with Mark. I did not often lose my temper with him directly, although that did happen four or five times in those last months, but I did deliberately let him see how stressed I was. I wanted him to know. Now do you see? Do you see how I am suffering on your account? One day, we were expecting the delivery of a new hospital bed for Mark. This one would be height-adjustable, and make it possible for him to sit up in bed with his head and shoulders supported. It would have an air mattress automatically varying the pressure under him, so he would not get bed sores: a modern, technological solution to the problem that the carers of Man Bac 9 had faced. Mark had taken the call from the delivery people and arranged, without consulting me, for them to bring the new bed that same afternoon. This meant that his old bed would have to be taken apart and moved out of the way, into the garage. This had to happen in the next couple of hours, before they arrived, so there would be space for the new bed, and there was nobody except me to do it. I got Mark into his wheelchair, stripped the bed and took apart the frame, but manoeuvring the king-size mattress out of the room, down the stairs and into the garage was too hard. I tried to balance it on its side, but it kept flopping heavily over – with me underneath, trying to hold it straight and push it up again. It was far heavier than I expected. It toppled sideways into one of the wall lights, smashing the bulb and knocking the whole fixture out of the wall, leaving the light hanging by wires, broken plaster and torn wallpaper. Now there was something else I would have to fix, and I did not know how – and why should this be my job? Other women of my age were not in this situation. My rage could have melted plastic. I was furious and tearful, swearing at the mattress, the light, my life, and, spitefully glad that Mark had to witness me not coping, I was performing a meltdown to make a point. See what you have done to me, accepting a delivery time when the children are not around to help, and no time to find a friend or relative? Do you see what I have to put up with, see what my life is like now, because of you? It is not reasonable to expect me to handle all this. It is not fair. Mark just sat there silently – for what could he do or say? – while I howled and raged. Oh, the spectacle of me! I wish I had acted with more grace.

Most of the time, though, when I remembered, when I had the energy to keep on, I managed to play my part. The key, I realized, was not what I felt, but what I did. My mantra came from *Sense and Sensibility*. When Marianne finds out that her sister Elinor has known for several months that Edward – the man she, Elinor, loves – is engaged to somebody else, but has respected the confidence in which she was told that information and has never complained, Marianne asks her how she has been able to bear it.

'By feeling that I was doing my duty.'

In Elinor's case, her duty was dictated by her promise to a friend, and a wish to spare her mother and sister any distress on her account. For me, doing my duty was looking after Mark and the children. I might feel bitter, frustrated and hopeless, but I could still be responsible for making everyone's meals, earning money for us, doing the laundry, ensuring that Mark had his medication, that his physical needs were met. I could rub cream into his back, help him to wash and dress, take care of his toileting. I could go to the supermarket and the pharmacy, make appointments, take the children to their activities and keep on top of what they needed for school. I could read to Mark and chat with him, though I did not spend as much time doing those things as he would have liked. By feeling that I was doing my duty, I could go on, through the hurt and the anger, and the worry. In films and books, what sustains people in dark times is love. I could not always manage love, but there was still duty. And there are stories and compassion.

With time, I found that, though I could not change how I felt, I could often control how I behaved. I imagined myself as I wanted to be, performed as if for an audience, and often that was enough. I costumed myself for the play I was acting in. I rehearsed my lines, adopted a face of patience and devotion. I am Carton, I am Elinor. My acting was superb, the finest in the sixth-form drama society. I could stay in character for hours, sometimes even days at a time. I developed a repertory of forbearance, of self-sacrifice. I hoped that the audience would applaud. I craved their good reviews.

19

GRAVE BJ581

The boys are playing chess. Adam is better and usually wins, but not always. Greg is nearly as good, and their games tend to be close – never the outright massacres that I remember suffering in games against my, embarrassingly younger, brother when I was a child. The chessboard is marquetry: looping, cryptic walnut around the edge and for the dark squares; the light squares are made of pale wood, perfectly fitted and smooth as paper. The wooden pieces which go with it are kept in a wooden box with a sliding lid and a peeling paper label, like an old-fashioned pencil box. Mark was given the set as a child – perhaps by his uncle? I do not quite remember, but he must have told me. Mark's name is written inside the lid of the box in a hand I do not recognize. It might be his father's.

I assumed that Mark would be exceptionally good at chess, because he drank his coffee black and listened to modern jazz. The first time we played, sitting across from each other at a tiny Formica-topped kitchen table barely bigger than the board, by the Rayburn in the house in Wales, I thought the game would be soon over. To my surprise, we were reasonably well matched, and neither of us very good. For Mark, the pleasure of playing chess was not only in the strategy, but also in the tactile and material engagement with his chess set. He ran his fingers lightly over the edge of the board as we played. I noticed that sometimes, when he took a piece, rather than put it in the usual PoW camp by the side of the board, he would sit and stroke the curves and angles of the wood.

Adam and Greg are better chess players than either of their parents. Occasionally, one of them plays a game online with a friend, but both prefer the ritual of getting the board down from the cupboard, taking the pieces out of the box and setting them up. For them, the game is a proper competition, but the board is also a material link to their father. The word 'heirloom' meant, originally, a thing or tool (*loom*, in Middle English) passed to one's heirs. Archaeologists often recover objects from graves and usually assume that they had some meaning for or relationship with the person who was buried there. One of the questions we have still not satisfactorily answered is what grave goods *meant*. For a question that is so fundamental, it is one that is rarely asked. Sometimes people assume that objects placed in a grave are for use in the next life; but sometimes they seem to say something about who that person was in this one.

In 1878, Swedish archaeologist Hjalmar Stolpe excavated several of the thousands of graves in the cemeteries around the Viking-age site of Birka. Birka was a trading town that flourished in the late first millennium; it is still one of the best known and most important sites for medieval

Scandinavia. One of the graves excavated by Stolpe, Bj581, had especially rich and high-status grave goods. Under a mound, inside a wooden chamber, were the skeletal remains of one person. Also in the grave were a spear, a sword, an axe, shields, a game board, dice and gaming pieces. Besides these, there were at least twenty-five arrowheads, lances and a knife. The fabric of the mound included more than 300 knives, and the very platform on which the burial sat was partially composed of lanceheads. This was quite the arsenal. Accompanying the single human burial, itself richly dressed in a cap trimmed with silver ornaments, were the remains of two horses, one of which had riding tack. Bj581 was one of the richest graves at Birka. It was the only one to have a whole suite of weapons, and was located in a high-status part of the site. Given the horses, arrows and weapons, this grave was usually interpreted as that of an elite warrior, possibly a mounted archer. Then, in 2017, Charlotte Hedenstierna-Jonson published her analysis of the genomic and isotopic information contained in the bones, confirming something that detailed osteological analysis had already suggested a few years previously, and causing an international stir: the warrior was female.

For nearly 140 years, archaeologists, historians and the numerous non-professional groups who love 'Vikings' had assumed that the occupant of Bj581 was male because, in the absence of good osteological or genetic sexing, attributing sex on the basis of grave goods was common practice. Plenty of people had pointed out the problems in making those assumptions – there have been good feminist critiques in archaeology for fifty years now – but, until recently, better methods were too difficult or expensive, so people carried on just the same. In the case of Viking-period burials, the wisdom was, weapons mean men; jewellery and domestic items mean women. But there are whole layers of meaning and complexity that determine what goes into a grave. Are grave goods the personal belongings of the deceased? Are they symbolic things or items necessary for some afterlife journey? Are they things that were meaningful to the bereaved? Or are they just incidental extras: the durable parts of whatever the deceased had been wearing, or a pot that had contained beer for the funeral meal that ended up in the grave? Grave goods are complicated and resist easy inter-pretation. Take that game board. Was it a thing that the occupant of the grave might enjoy in the hereafter? Or a tribute to her strategic abilities? Was it a thing that had belonged to her? Game boards are reasonably well known from burials of this period, usually with higher status, appar-ently male burials, but then, this grave was apparently male too; perhaps, when we do the tests, we will find many other female burials with game boards.

People still put grave goods into the coffins of their dead, though not so often. Maybe a piece of jewellery, a favourite piece of clothing. I have heard of one person buried in the tatty old fishing hat he liked to wear, and another buried in a pair of bunny slippers. Mostly, though, we do not bury or burn the most meaningful things; these days, we keep them.

The chess set the boys are playing with is the descendant of the board and pieces in Bj581. It was Mark's. Now it stays on top of the cupboard in the front room, close to the place we keep the Dad Box, a crate full of cards and letters, newspaper clippings, old school magazines, things the boys might want to see. It also has Baby Bear, his childhood toy, about fifteen centimetres tall and almost bald. I do not keep any of his letters to me, nor mine to him, nor any of the gifts that passed between us, in the Dad Box. They still feel too personal for the children to have, but perhaps, when we are all older, I will put them in. For now, the Dad Box is a kind of cenotaph, a tomb without a body, but a place of remembering, nonetheless.

20

A HISTORY OF FALSE TEETH

The winter before I began my PhD, I was in India. This was excavation as the grand imperial adventurers of the 1930s might have known it. I half expected Indiana Jones to come striding past the row of tents. The trained professionals, almost all of whom worked for the Archaeological Survey of India, were accommodated in large tents furnished with proper beds, desks and bathtubs, to which servants brought hot water twice a day. Our days were spent recording finds and drawing sections at a large, multi-period site in eastern Maharashtra. Labourers from the village were employed by the day to dig the trenches and care for our comfort. Their tasks included the daily re-chalking of the badminton court behind our tents, cooking our meals and bringing out cups of chai to us on site, sometimes with sweet, oily jalebis to munch on.

The labourers' village was only a couple of hundred metres from the site and our camp, but I had not visited until one Saturday morning, just before lunch. Something was happening. I could hear a band crashing badly through Hindi pop music: 'Ek Do Teen', the ubiquitous hit of the previous year. Looking over, there seemed to be a press of people in colourful clothes.

On the edge of the crowd, children chased one another or sat playing with toys on the ground. Nosiness pulled me along the dusty track that separated our camp from the village. As I got closer, I could see that people had cups and sweets in their hands and were passing them around to each other, to the insatiable children – and to me, as I approached. There was something at the centre of the throng, towards which most of the people were facing. It must be a religious festival, I thought. There will be a statue of a god in the middle, dressed for the feast, with flowers and perfume. I edged through the crowd to take a closer look. At the heart of the laughing, chattering, sweet-eating party was a bier, bearing the body of an elderly woman under heaps of marigolds and cotton. I had shouldered my way through family, friends and neighbours to the front row of a stranger's funeral. I was horrendously embarrassed. How awful that I had gatecrashed such an intimate occasion, gawping and stuffing sweets into my gob. Red faced, I stammered my apologies and turned to leave. The man I spoke to – one of the workmen I recognized from the site – did not understand me, but another man reassured me. I had not upset anyone; everyone was welcome. The dead woman was old enough to have known her grandchildren; this was not a sad death. I had assumed I knew what a funeral was, what the appropriate public emotional expression for bereavement should be, and I was wrong on both counts.

My bereavement is not just about grief, and my experience does not seem to be what other people expect me to be experiencing. I feel like I am getting widowhood wrong.

A couple of months after Mark died, I was more tired than I had imagined possible, drained of all energy and barely able to drag us through the days, doing just enough shopping, cooking and cleaning to keep us alive and avoid the unwanted attention of social services. We were all still exhausted by illness and death and the events of the year, so I decided to take the children to Crete for a week, and I booked no improving activities or cultural trips. Our only plan was to swim, read books, sleep, eat and play cards, and that is what we did. I read seven books in seven days. One of them was the memoir of neurosurgeon Paul Kalanithi, *When Breath Becomes Air*. Kalanithi was a neurosurgeon who was diagnosed with lung cancer when he was thirty-six. He was clearly an exceptional man, with a passion for literature and philosophy as well as medicine, a fistful of degrees in different subjects. It would be easy to roll your eyes at his apparently perfect life and Olympian personal success. But you do not and you cannot, because against all of that golden good fortune is the one big fact that, just as his life was opening up, he got terminal cancer and died.

I wonder whether all neurosurgeons are like him: exceptionally driven, intelligent, wide-ranging, humanistic. I think of the writer and brain surgeon Henry Marsh, for example. Maybe their work brings them forcibly to consider matters of life and death, what makes people themselves and what makes us human at all. I remember seeing Dr Leite in action – her exceptional devotion to her work and her patients goes beyond most. During Mark's in-patient stays in the John Radcliffe, he noticed how often she was there first thing in the morning and last thing at night, and how she was there at weekends. I do not know if she had a partner or family, but, if she did, I don't imagine they got to see her much.

And what would I say to Dr Leite if I were to write to her now? First, I would thank her. Mark was the most cynical man I ever met, but even he was moved to tears to think of the time she gave us, of how responsive she was to our out-of-hours contacts. She and Mary Quirke, the specialist nurse, called us at home to check how things were going. She gave me her personal phone number. But I would also like to raise the issue of prognosis and uncertainty. As Paul Kalanithi says, how can you plan when you don't have any idea about how long you've got? A year? Two years? Ten? And, of course, I appreciate that, even when the cause of a disease is known and its general progression is well documented, it is not possible to predict the course of an individual and specific case – not usually, anyway. But I think we would have been able to handle the last few years better if we had known authoritatively what to expect, or even the range of possible outcomes and by what signs we would know if we were on our way back to the main road, or if we were going to end our journey out in the woods somewhere. Instead, we were lurching about in the dark, tripping over tree roots, and not sure what direction we were going in, or what it would look like when we got there. At those times, doctors are our maps and compasses, but we had neither.

Most of all, I would want to share with her my dismay at a medical system which sees the preservation of life as the paramount goal, in all but the direst of situations. I would want to give voice to my anger that a tyranny of protocols and best practices is in place to identify 'suicide risk' and prevent anyone from taking control of their own life's ending. Not all suicide is the result of mental aberration. But the equation of suicide with psychopathology leads to a singular, medicalized view of it as an end that should at all costs be prevented. It is part of our society's futile and irrational war on death. Death, in any case, cannot be prevented, only postponed.

Because Mark's entirely rational desire to avoid extending his life into a long tail of pain, depression, degradation, uselessness (as he saw it), boredom, loss of intellectual acuity and immobility was regarded as pathological, we could get no support with the single biggest issue he faced. Because, if it were known that I suspected what he was planning, I would be criminally culpable of failing to stop him, we had to maintain a fiction that our discussions of how you approach the end of life, and whether there are things you can do to control how that end happens, were impersonal and intellectual only, that they did not relate to a real plan. And, most of all, most of all, I am angry that he had to die alone, when I would have loved, and he would have wanted, for us to be together at that hardest and loneliest moment of his life, with me holding his hand, talking about his life and our life together, thanking him for all our years and for what he had done for us, reassuring him that the kids and I would not forget him, but that we would be all right. I had little enough to offer at the end, but I might have given him whatever was left of the glue that had held us together and brought us that far: stories and compassion.

Nothing divides a life like the death of a partner. On second thoughts, maybe having your first child does. Like becoming a mother, the event of your partner's death is more than just an episode, even a super-emotional episode. It affects your whole life in such pervasive ways that it becomes a kind of frontier – a line that separates before from after, a thing which makes it hard to see from one side to the other, which can make the bereaved feel cut off from the continent of their friends whose relationships are still intact. This is something different to just emotional pain. When my father died, I felt terrible grief; my emotions were profoundly affected. They still are, and I miss him every day. But my life was not much altered. I did not need to change my working hours, my financial arrangements or my relationship with my children. It did not change my friendships, challenge my values or shake my confidence. I was deeply sad, but mostly able, after the funeral, to go on as before, albeit being more active in looking after my mother. When Mark died, though, everything changed. It was a *terminus post quem*. I was now the only person taking care of the children, and knew this would be the ongoing situation, which had real consequences. I could not go out when they were home from school, because there was nobody to take care of them. Even when he was bedridden, Mark had at least been an adult presence in the house so that I could pop out to run errands. For the same reason, there were many parts of my job that

I could no longer manage. Being a professor normally requires you to go to conferences and meetings, but, when I became unable to leave my children overnight because of Mark's illness, that kind of work was no longer practical. Now, it would be years before I could go away alone again. I negotiated to continue my part-time hours.

So, there I was, on my forty-ninth birthday, sitting on a rock by the Mediterranean, two months after Mark's death, listening to the waves, like the cover photo from a meditation app or self-help website, but fatter. And I felt . . . what? Not exactly sad, though there was much grief and sorrow, which mainly took the form of pity and admiration for Mark, and regret that I did not tell him what he needed to hear, and now I never can. I worried that I was fluffing my lines, not doing widowhood right, muddling things up, getting the order wrong. Immediately after his death, I thought mainly about my future and that of my children, not so much about Mark. But, two and a half months on, I thought about him a lot. I dreamed about him most nights. Often, I dreamed that he was not really dead – there had been some mistake, and now there was a great muddle because we had already held the funeral and got on with life as though he were no longer in it. I needed to get his clothes back and contact the bank to see if we could reopen his account. Pretty much my last thought every night was of Mark's death. I relived dozens of times that scene of me coming into the house and shouting, 'Hello, I'm home!' Then, 'Mark?' And the silence. Oh, darling. I'd tear up and try to get a grip. My sorrow was for what he had to go through, for his physical suffering and his emotional pain. But it was not, at that point, because I missed him. I did not – or not yet. I missed the kind of life I had hoped I might have, the kind of close, loving family bonds we could have had, but our family life had not felt like that for a long time. Emotional bonds tied me to the children and them to each other, but Mark was never very much part of that web. Now, more than ever, the children and I were a tight little unit of four.

Sometimes I felt a lurching anxiety about how I would manage on my own. I cried in the middle of the night, quietly, so as not to wake the children. Sometimes these were tears of anxiety and dislocation, being alone and having to face a future of being alone, but more often, now, when I thought of my future, I also felt relief at the freedom and independence that widowhood and some material security had given me. There was also fear, because mortality and decay had surrounded me to such an extent that my own death – or, more likely and worse, dementia – felt close. I had lived too long among the dead and dying, and the chances that I would myself be alive and present for my children as they grew up sometimes seemed slim.

I often forgot for hours at a stretch that anything had happened. But at other times it enveloped me utterly. I wanted to shout in the faces of people I passed on the street or stood next to in the queue at the library, 'Don't you know what has happened to me? MY HUSBAND HAS DIED! And I'm only in my forties! And I have young children!' At this moment, two and a half months after his death, that seemed like the most significant thing about me. The grass had not begun to grow over the open hole of our bereavement; the process of backfilling had barely begun. But I remember feeling that way when I was first pregnant, and then when Rachel was born: 'Don't you know I'm a MOTHER? I have a tiny BABY, and she came out of my body!' In time, those bits of biography became just part of the normal experience of being me – not the most important things, though still meaningful parts of my identity. So, in time, I hoped that my widowhood would recede a little in my own sense of self, and it would be just another thing that happened in my past. I considered how eventful my life had been, and recently even melodramatic; it all seemed a bit overblown, maybe not in very good taste. When I was a child, I used to hope that my life would be full of events and adventures – not just great achievements and happy holidays, but also emotional intensity, all sorts of people and relationships. I never wanted a life that was all sunshine, tulips and custard. That is not living, or not living richly. Not living a textured life. I wanted to know how things felt – extraordinary things, unusual things, as well as lovely ones. In *Swimming with Seals*, Victoria Whitworth talks about her need to reclaim primal fears – of dark and dangerous creatures, of unknown depths, of, ultimately, death itself. Not to vanquish those fears, but to chart them. I am a worried person. I worry about the future, about my family, my health, their health, whether we will have enough money, whether the boiler will break down again, that noise the car is making. I worry most of all that people I love will die. I rehearse the possible ways that might happen, not so much to be better prepared, or for any practical purpose, but just because I can't not think about it. I need to chart the territory, plumb the sea floor for hidden reefs and trenches.

And so – I suppose I am getting what I wished for. A life with too much experience is better than one with too little. My life – the ridiculous, unlikely sparrow's flight of it – is so precarious, so limited, I want to fill it with whatever might be available, and that includes tragedy, grief, frustration, as well as joy and exhilaration. It would be months, or maybe years before I knew how the last few years had affected me, what I had gained and what I had lost. I still do not know. When the ground has settled into its new geography, when I have moulded the emotions, the boredom, the time it all took, forgotten some events, reordered or improved others, crafted a set of good narratives, how will I emerge? And really, still, how will I be? It would be satisfying if I came out more compassionate, more tolerant, wiser, better able to cope with stress and disappointment. But what if I come out perma-nently cynical, doubting that love can ever last, impatient with the trivial problems of people who are not facing death or devastation? What if there is too little time left to me to find out *how* I emerge before I myself succumb to dementia, or cancer, or a cross-current that is stronger than I foresaw? I dreamed I was dying. In my dream, I said, 'Thank you for letting me live.' But I do not know to whom I was talking.

By the time we got to Crete, I had been Mark's widow more than five times as long as I was his wife. But having been, however briefly, his wife, I could now legitimately call myself his widow. His death had constructed new characters out of both of us. I had become the tragic, young widow, whose grief other people think they know. All the sympathy cards and letters sent by old friends, relatives, good friends and people I did not know constructed a slightly different Mark. Not wrong, not somebody else, but a subtly different, maybe partial one. To use John Bunyan's metaphor for the resurrection of the dead, he was 'candied fruit', the essence recognizably him, but made sweet, bright and shining. And I was not above doing something similar, I realized, creating a narrative of Mark that was all about his last phase and his death. Jackie Kay's novel, *Trumpet*, another book I read during that week on Crete, is about a Black, Scottish jazz musician, who is revealed, after his death at the age of seventy, to have been biologically a woman, living as a man, married and with an adopted son. We only see the main character, Joss, through other people's accounts and impressions of him. It is about the grief of the widow, who just wants to be treated like a widow and not be a participant in a scandal; about his son, who feels betrayed and furious; and about a gutter journalist, who wants to write and sell a sensationalized version of his life. Kay's regular themes, also central to this story, are identity, race and gender. For me, it was also about the way in which you can make new stories, and new identities, for people after their death. In that case, Joss could become something in the journalist's story that was nothing like him in life. He could become she.

I realized, in Crete, that I'd had enough of death and dying. I wanted to be in the world of the living for a bit. I resolved that my next research project would not be about death. I might come back to it later, but, just for now, I wanted my research to perch not on bones, but on the things of the living. I made a few notes about a possible new project on the history of false teeth. That seemed cheerful. My new philosophy was to be taken from a line of Paul Kalanithi's. 'If the unexamined life was not worth living,' he asked, 'was the unlived life worth examining?' I watched the children messing about in the sea, healthy and vital. I tried to pay attention to how my lungs filled with air, to the smell of the suncream, the noise of voices and waves and Europop from somebody's phone speaker. I needed to keep the darkness away with things that were powerful and immediate, with little syrupy pastries and the heat of the sun on my face, with my children laughing because Greg, for a dare, had allowed Rachel to shave off one of his eyebrows.

Rationally, I did not feel any guilt. Rationally, I knew that ending his own life was the best thing for Mark in that situation, but at another level I wondered if I should have tried harder to keep him alive. Should I have tried to persuade him not to take steps on his own? Should I have made sure he was supervised, and not left him alone that night? Oh, Mark. I comfort myself that I did my duty, that I stayed with him and took care of him, even at times when he was not very kind to me and I did not much like him. I also said cruel things to him and I was angry. I let him know that caring for him was coming at a cost to me. I made sure he saw how much I struggled with taking care of the house, garden and family on my own. If I had known it would not be for much longer, I think I could have been kinder. On the other hand, I tell myself, I could have been, wanted to be, much worse. I wanted to run away at times, but I stayed. I cared for him, talked with him, managed his treatments, missed out on many opportunities for me and the children, feeling that I was doing my duty. I allowed my life to be shaped by his needs: my home, my career, how I spent my time. I put up with a lot. I am not the villain in this. And neither was he. He was a man under unbearable strain. The price he paid was in no way proportionate. It was just unfair.

On the day we returned from Crete, Rachel gave me a book. It was a recently published volume of short stories that Mark had given to her a few months earlier, with instructions to give it to me for my birthday. It looked like just the sort of thing I would enjoy. In the front, he has written, *To Sarah. Happy birthday or whatever . . . Lots of love and thank you for everything, Mark.* I cried, because it was such a nice thing, and because he had planned for not being around, and because that is not a message of bitterness or blame. It felt like forgiveness.

21

SECONDARY DEPOSITS

In one of the letters he left on the night he died, Mark asked that his body be given to the researchers at the John Radcliffe, so I arranged for the hospital to collect his body after the post-mortem and take it to Oxford. We never really discussed the details, Dr Leite and I, so I thought that they would take his whole body and I did not expect to hear back from them. I went ahead and organized a bodyless funeral at Leicester Guildhall, where we had music and speaking, followed by lots of food and drink. Then, when that had all happened, I was surprised to get a phone call asking me what I wanted to do with Mark's body. It turned out that the John Radcliffe had only taken his brain and spinal cord; the rest was still in the care of the county coroner. We had already had a funeral and I felt that the Guildhall event had been our formal goodbye to Mark. We did not want another collective ritual event. I felt somewhat flustered by this turn of events, and I could feel the welling-up of my customary anxiety that, by not doing the orthodox things, I had, again, screwed up. Mark's body, what was left of it, had become problematic stuff. I had read about David Bowie, who had died not long before Mark, having a plain, non-ceremonial cremation, so

I called a company that specializes in cremation without funerals. They find end-of-line or wrongly ordered coffins that might otherwise be wasted, and arrange for bodies to be cremated without ceremony or service, using spare capacity at any crematorium in the region. They arranged for the rest of Mark's body to be cremated in Derbyshire. A few days later, I drove to the crematorium to collect what are known in the profession as the cremains, but were referred to politely by the crematorium receptionist on the phone as the remains of my loved one.

Three years earlier, during my training as a humanist celebrant, I had taken a backstage tour of a crematorium near Coventry. When the coffin disappears from view behind a curtain, or on a conveyor belt that takes it out of the chapel, it does not go directly into the oven. Usually, the bodies are burned in the evening, after the day's funerals are over. The crematorium operators slide the coffin into a furnace, and it is incinerated until all wood, flesh and most bone has been consumed. When the ashes are cool enough, a large magnet picks out any lumps of metal (implants, coffin fittings and so on) and the remaining substantial solids are put through a grinding 'cremulator', which pulverizes the lumps and shards of bone so that the resulting dust does not look too anatomical.

When I collected Mark's remains from the crematorium, the woman on the reception desk fetched for me a big cream cardboard box, which she opened to show that it contained a quantity of white and grey grit in a plastic bag. Mark. She closed the box again and put it in a sort of reinforced gift bag, the kind of thing we might have received wedding presents in, if we'd had that sort of a wedding, if there had been presents. It was surprisingly heavy. I thought of Philip Larkin's line, always quoted out of context to saccharine effect: 'What will survive of us is love.' But what also survives is about six pounds, or 3.5 per cent of the person's original weight. I came across a table online that gave the weight and volume of cremated ashes to help bereaved people choose an urn of the right size. It had a section giving the weight of ashes for a child's body, sorted by age and sex, so you could find that, for a twelve-year-old girl, you'd need an urn with a capacity of 2.25 litres. God.

I drove home with Mark on the passenger seat. It was a hot day. My memory of May, June and July 2016 is that they were all hot days. I took a random turn off the A-road and drove aimlessly along small country lanes until I came to a wood, where I pulled onto an overgrown verge. Leaving Mark in the car, I climbed over the fence and walked through the wood, following a small brook upstream, until I came out into a sloping field, bordered on the other side by a long turf gallop. I sat on the grass in the sunshine, watching the butterflies. I found that I was sitting in a patch of clover with a lot of four-leafers, so I picked some, planning to give them to the kids. I felt happy in the warm sun, and then anxious that it was not appropriate that the occasion of driving my husband's ashes home should be a moment of sunshine, butterflies and four-leafed clovers. Back at the car, I popped one of them in Mark's bag. A cremation assemblage.

At home, I set the gift bag on the kitchen table. Mark and

I had never discussed scattering ashes. I thought about places that had been special to us, but I also thought about when my friend Alex's father had died and how he'd asked for his ashes to be scattered in the hills he had loved in his youth, some distance from where his widow or either of his children now lived. Alex had said he was sorry there was no place where his father would notionally 'be', where Alex could go and talk to him, perhaps bringing a fiancée or a child there in the future. A couple of years earlier, I had interviewed a tattoo artist in Leicester who specialized in memorial tattoos, mixing some of a relative's or pet's ashes into the tattoo ink and using that to make a portrait or write some words on the bereaved. I liked the idea of Mark's memory being literally written into my skin, but I am not really a tattoo kind of person. In the meantime, I put the bag of ashes in the top of the wardrobe, next to the winter bedspread and the old dressing gown I wear when I dye my hair.

In the end, the children and I scattered half his ashes in the little river that ran past the first house we shared in Wales, and the other half closer to us, in a patch of woodland we had endowed in his memory. The Woodland Trust put up a memorial post there, and I have been back a few times, each time glad to be able to talk to him – though, stumbling about, gesticulating and tearfully remonstrating with a wooden post, I am carefully ignored by the dog-walkers who occasionally happen by.

In Bronze Age Germany, the ashes of the cremated dead were sometimes collected and put into special cremation urns. The urns have faces on them and look like little proxy people. When archaeologists carried out minute excavations of the contents of the urns, they found that, where bone elements were recognizable – as bits of leg bone, vertebrae, skull or whatever – they appeared in the anatomically correct position relative to the other elements inside the vessel: toe bones at the bottom, cranial fragments at the top. The ashes had been put into the urns with care, preserving the closest approximation of the living body. More than three thousand years ago, people had fashioned a simulacrum of the dead person, out of clay and ashes. I understand the impulse. The anthropologist Alfred Gell talks about 'exuviae', the things that do the work of a person, the traces and productions that go out into the world and stand for that person. Mark's exuviae include his published writing; the gifts, photos and keepsakes in the Dad Box; his chess board and the other grave goods that never saw a grave. Those Bronze Age cremation urns were exuviae or agents of that kind, and so is the memorial post among the trees at Woodhall Spa.

Bereavement is worse after a suicide death, wrote one of the friends in her sympathy card, *because you must be feeling so much guilt and anger.* I did not think I was, at that time, feeling either of those things. The anger that had been my constant companion over the last few years had finally gone, because who was there to be angry with now? And, if Mark had anything to atone for, what more could he do? I felt no desire to act out old grudges, no need to drag out his remains and splat my boat on top of them. Thus, for the first time in years, I did not feel resentment constricting my throat and tensing my shoulders. Instead, there was just an empty exhaustion, a listlessness that left me fit only for reading fiction or watching TV for hours, in between bursts of energetic organizing. I could only organize straightforward things, though. It took about a year before I felt like doing anything hard. I think my desire for action, to be sorting things out, came from the same place as the big post-miscarriage photo sort: a drive to do something, to take control of something in a situation I was powerless to control.

And guilt? My card-writing friend is not the only one who expects the suicide survivor to feel guilt. A review of professional advice to psychiatrists highlights that the inclination to find a person to blame for a suicide death is common: targets might be the dead person themselves, the doctor who missed something, a friend or relative who is perceived to have been insufficiently supportive or in some way responsible for pushing the suicidal person over the edge, but, most commonly, the therapist should expect the bereaved person to blame themselves. Self-blame is, apparently, very common, and with it comes guilt. Survivors pick over their interactions with the suicide, counsellors are taught. They will wonder, What could I have done differently? Did I fail to notice how serious things had become? Was I argumentative, unkind, impatient? Was it my words that pushed him over the edge? If we had not been so grumpy that morning, if I had remembered to kiss him goodbye and tell him I loved him, if I had not gone out and left him to be sucked under by the whirlpool of his despair, whatever. From what I observe in the Bereaved By Suicide Facebook group, however, guilt/self-blame is not the issue that is most discussed among survivors themselves – that is not guilt, but stigma. It is not feeling guilty that is the worst thing, it is the feeling that other people think you *should* feel guilty. In other words, my friend's card, though written no doubt with the kindest of intentions, and meant only to show understanding, succeeded in making me feel worse. Did she think I *ought* to be feeling guilt? Did she think I was to blame? Was the death of my husband to be understood as my failure to keep him alive?

Greg, fatherless two days after his eleventh birthday, showed remarkable empathy in dealing with Mark's death. 'I'm comforted to know that Dad chose to die,' he said to me. 'That's better than thinking that he wanted to be alive and couldn't.'

I do not feel guilty, though I wonder if I ought to. Because I could have tried to prevent his suicide. I knew he was thinking of it. I could have checked his post and searched his bedside cabinet. I could have made sure he never got the package containing the pentobarbital. I could have worked it so that he was never alone in the house. I could have begged him not to.

I can make no claim that I have nothing to feel guilty for or nothing to be ashamed of. I have plenty of those. But Mark did not die because of me, and, in any case, I decided I would not accept that his death was a tragedy that I should have averted by being more vigilant or getting psychological help for him. I am defiant in the face of this stigma. I want people to know how he died and why. I am proud of Mark and of his courage.

Part of the problem is that there is no word for Mark's kind of death. It was not assisted dying, because he did not get any assistance. Maybe we need a different word than suicide. Mark was no suicide, I wanted to say to the card-writing friend. His death was not an act of evasion or despair, although hope was certainly gone from us at that point. His was an act of courage and of love. Say 'suicide' and people think of the desperate act of an otherwise healthy individual succumbing to severe depression. It is tragic because, with the right help, this kind of suicide should not be inevitable: their depression could have been treated, their circumstances improved and they could have enjoyed many more years of happy life. Another young widow friend of mine has a properly tragic story of this kind. Her husband developed a gambling addiction, which he hid even from those closest to him. To pay his debts, he took money that did not belong to him. Some money was borrowed from friends and relatives under false pretences, other funds were taken from a club in his village. Of course, he was unable to pay it back. Soon, the accounts needed to be examined and he knew his theft was about to be discovered. He told nobody what had happened or what trouble he was in, not even his wife. Instead, he travelled to Whitby and jumped off the high cliff, south of the abbey. My friend recalls her increasing panic that afternoon when her husband sent her a final text directing her to a note he had left on her pillow. He was not answering his phone and she was beginning to feel the dread that something awful had happened, but tried anyway to attend their son's parents' evening. Noticing how anxious and preoccupied she was, her son's head teacher took control of calling family and the police. The husband's body was found that night. A farmer had seen him disappear from the cliff path and called the coastguard, otherwise his body might never have been recovered. After his death, his financial situation and the extent of his deceit came to light. The money involved was, in the end, written off. Eleven years later, my friend's grief and frustration is still raw. 'We could have sorted it,' she says. The chair of the cricket club, from which he had taken some cash, told her, 'To start with, I was angry when I found out what he had done. But then I thought, We have lost some money, but your son has lost his father and your husband has lost his life.' They were robbed of a future that could still have been saved.

For those in Mark's situation, that is not the case. Nine months later, at Mark's inquest, the coroner considered the reports from the police officer who attended the call, from the pathologist and the toxicologist who examined Mark's body, and my own account of his situation and the events around his death. A few weeks before the inquest, the coroner had sent me the pathologist's report, which concluded, bizarrely, that Mark had died of natural causes, specifically heart failure. This was flummoxing. How can a man decide to end his own life, take a powerful drug to make this happen, and then, coincidentally, die of a pre-existing but undiagnosed heart condition? It took a couple of months to clear that one up. It turned out that nobody had told the pathologist about Mark's circumstances. To her knowledge, this was an unexplained death in bed. Death by pentobarbital is so unusual that there is no standard way to quantify its concentration in the human body. Even forensic toxicologists would only look for it if specifically asked to do so. A routine post-mortem looks only for the more usual causes of death. This pathologist had found that Mark's heart was in a poor state: congestion severe enough that death from heart failure was a reasonable conclusion. If Mark had not died deliberately that night, his heart might well have given up anyway in the next few weeks or months.

I was dreading the inquest, though I had seen all the reports in advance, so there was little to surprise me. The Lincolnshire coroner's court meets in a serious, panelled room, in a building close to Lincoln cathedral. My sister-in-law Susan and I were the only family participants and, on the appointed morning, the courtroom was mostly empty: just the expert witnesses, the coroner, his assistant and a scribe. And Susan and me. The expert witnesses presented their own reports, but my statement was read out by a courtroom assistant. I suppose they are used to relatives being too upset to speak. And then, as expected, the coroner announced that he would be recording a verdict of death by suicide. It felt so wrong to me, like there was no difference between Mark's death and a man jumping off a cliff because his role in a financial scandal was about to be revealed, or hanging himself in the garage because he could not see a way out of his depression. When the coroner asked me if I was satisfied with the verdict, I told him that I understood why he had reached it, but I voiced my frustration that the specific circumstances of his death would be misrepresented by the word 'suicide'. The sympathetic coroner understood immediately why I felt ambivalent about a suicide verdict, and offered to change it for what is called a narrative verdict, a short account of events leading to a death, without attributing it directly to one of the shorthand causes of death that normally feature on a death certificate. Mark's registered cause of death, for the purposes of the register and of the collection of statistics, is suicide, but the coroner's record will have a bit more nuance.

When I meet people now who do not know our history, I tend to say that Mark died because he had a progressive neurological condition. It is a little misleading, but to say suicide is equally misleading. We need a new word, another story.

Suicide can be rational. Being dead is sometimes better than being alive. Sometimes we honour a life by letting it end, and by being present in that moment to hold a hand, to remember a love, to report him and his cause aright.

I do not feel guilty, but I do wish things had been different. Now that I have arranged the time of Mark's illness and death into a story, I wish the character of me was a bit nicer. I wish I had behaved both more kindly and more confidently, and I do not quite remember why I did not. At every stage, I wish I had done things better. Why did I let our relationship go sour? If I had been able to be more assertive, could I have strengthened our love, better braced it for the storm when it came?

And, at the end, I wish we had been more frank with each other. I wish Mark had been able to tell me what he planned to do, and I had been able to say goodbye properly.

I wish I had sat beside him when he died. I wish I had held his hand as he dropped from consciousness, from pain, from life. I wish he had heard me say, 'Thank you for your love, for your pride in me and the children. I am sorry for the times I failed you. Please forgive me. I forgive you for the times you failed me. Can we put behind us the countless little hurts we wrought upon one another? You have done good things with your life. You are loved. You will be remembered. I will do my best to make sure the children grow up happy, strong and fulfilled, and honour your memory. We will talk about you all the time. You have been so brave.

'Thank you. I am sorry. We have had good times, haven't we? We have loved each other, haven't we? Do you remember the bluebells, Mark?'

And I wish he had died remembering them, remembering us, astonished, transcendent, in the wood, with that saturated, radiant blue as far as we could see.

22

HUNTER-GATHERERS

I knew when I started writing this story that I was not confident in my memory. Already I have forgotten things. I am surprised sometimes by a photograph or a comment, and I think, Oh, yes. That's right. We did do that. Part of what made me want to write was the gradual and uneven fading of my own recollections. I see now that what I have done is mostly to write the bad years, the conflict, the pain, the pair of us at our worst. These are the memories I have made solid, building out with words, this is the narrative I have constructed. And already I am asking, Am I remembering that right? Some memories hurt to recall because they are so poignant, and the things lost are so absolutely gone that the grief is physical pain. Some of them feel horrible because I am ashamed of my own part, the things I said or did, or failed to do because I was too lazy or selfish or stupid. I was tempted to leave those out, or rewrite them to make my behaviour more gracious, or cool, or clever, or kind. I am aware that nobody is going to pull me up on either genuine mistakes or ingenuous mythologizing, and I am not sure I can be trusted. Trying to remember is, anyhow, boxing smoke. It is a problem for all of us who have looked death in the eye, and for those laid waste by bereavement. Memory is all I am, all Mark now is. Without memory, I am hardly a self at all, as I see with the progress of my mother's brutally relentless dementia. And, if you are not remembered, what kind of a self is left? A self in the things you have made, perhaps, in what you have passed on to your children, genetically and otherwise, and some bones or ashes. An academic paper, Adam's brown eyes, the word 'splonger' for a potato masher, a wooden chess set.

This is a story about compassion – its failure, its redemptive qualities, how it is frustrated and lost, and then maybe rediscovered. I wish I had been more patient. I wish I had been kinder. I wish I had been more like the kind of carer you read about in magazines, whose concern is always for the person they are caring for, who never thinks of their own frustrated hopes, who never locks herself into the bathroom so that she can cry without the children hearing. I wish I was the kind of person for whom love had been enough, but I am not and it was not. There are many ways to tell my part in this story: as victim, as villain, as tragic, romantic heroine. I do not think I know how to be fair to us both in constructing this account.

It has taken me time to remember that there was not just the anger and frustration of those last months, the way we hurt each other and suffered in our separateness, but that there was also love. Before any of it, there was love, and now, years after it all ended in that bed with the yellow duvet, on a sunny, warm May morning that failed spectacularly to befit itself to the momentous event, now, there it is again, coming up like a morning mushroom through the litter of our lives: love. I must remember how passionate and exciting it felt at the start, and the solid ordinariness of it through the years of young children, through the Christmases and the summer holidays and the cups of tea in bed. The thousands of meals prepared and eaten together, the dozens of times we listened to one another's familiar anecdotes and opinions, passing from rapt interest, through boredom, to a comfortable familiarity. There were moments of passion, of tenderness, of anger and regret, but mostly there were just days, months, years tumbling past, in a long, commonplace ordinary.

Mark loved these things: the hunter-gatherers of the Mesolithic, woods, food, getting things for free. Little brought him more pleasure than foraging for wild mushrooms on a damp day in autumn. His father had come to England as a young man, after the war. Witold Pluciennik was never what he called 'nationalized' into Britishness, but his Polish citizenship had been lost in the confusion of geography and history, leaving him stateless. Mark remembered the fuss of papers and visas every time the family travelled abroad. Their father told Mark and Susan little about the war. He preferred to reminisce about his early childhood, growing up in a mill house by the river. He spoke of going to school by sledge in the winter, of the creak of snow under his boots, and of watching kingfishers on the river. Like many rural Poles of his generation, he was easy with the natural world, and casually knowledgeable about its potentials. He knew which were the best edible mushrooms, and where to find them. He had learned to swim and skate as a child in the river next to his house. Where I had childhood memories of the puddled lino around the skate-hire desk at Solihull ice rink, Mark had been taught to skate by his father on the frozen ponds of Epping Forest. For me, mushrooms came from Tesco and came in two kinds: ordinary and chestnut. For him, there were mycological riches to be found everywhere. Mark never achieved his father's relaxed expertise with wild mushrooms, but he set himself to learn.

Taking bags and children, we made foraging trips to Old Dalby Wood, collecting everything. He hoped for ceps or morels, but we found instead strange, greenish-yellow venomous-looking slimepads, or more edible-seeming, brown, biscuity ones. There were bracket fungi, usually too old and woody to be worth picking, and miniature villages of tiny, cloche-hatted pixies. We collected them all to take home and identify in the big mushroom book. Most of them turned out to be poisonous, or were described in the book by the intriguing but scary tag, *Edibility unknown*. During his lifetime, Mark was more gung-ho than me about wild food. Back then, I was distrustful of fungi gathered in woods and fields. As a child, I had been told not to eat any kind of mushroom, unless it was bought in a shop. I remember our primary-school class being sat in front of the heavy TV that was wheeled in for our occasional education, to watch a public-information film about all the ways the British countryside was trying to kill us. A little group of children dwindled as they succumbed, one by one, to common, but mortal, bucolic dangers. As I recall it, one girl, who had survived being drowned in slurry or crushed by a tractor, fell victim to a beautiful but deadly destroying angel, mistaking it for a common field mushroom. I did not intend to go the same way, nor to allow any reckless gambling with the children's livers or indeed lives. Our arrangement was this: Mark would do his best to identify a find, including taking spore prints and whatever else was necessary. If he was reasonably sure that he had got it right, and there was no possible confusion with any of the really deadly kinds, he would cook and eat one or two. If he was still all right twelve hours later, the children and I could have it too.

Our best finds came not from the woods, but from closer to home. Our lawn turned out to have a ring of St George's mushrooms on it – tasty and abundant mushrooms that appear every year around the 23 April, hence their name, in honour of St George's Day. And in the front garden two doors along from us was the dead trunk of a tree on which bubbly yellow chicken-of-the-woods grew in profusion. Mark had forager's dreams. He wanted to find morels, with their pleated, honeycomb caps, or the celebrated penny bun mushrooms that the French call ceps and the Italians porcini. He told me that his father knew a place where they grow, but had refused to tell even his son the secret spot before he died. Most of all, Mark wanted to find a young and edible giant puffball. These huge white mushrooms can be as big as an exercise ball, and are pure white all the way through. You can fry them in batter, make soup or stew, or use them in almost any savoury dish. In culinary terms, they are like a kind of wild tofu. But the only ones Mark ever found were the sad, deflated late-season bags of brown spores – no good for eating.

The weird thing is, since his death, I have found myself stopping on walks to take a couple of steps backwards and look again at what I think I just saw. Was that a blewit, maybe, hiding coyly in the grass? Or a parasol, sticking its ruffed neck up among the scattered oaks in the park? Now, I am the one who keeps my pockets stuffed with plastic bags, just in case, or comes home with an unexpected haul of chanterelles in the hood of my jacket. It is me who takes the spore prints and smiles indulgently at nervous relatives who have reservations about my surprise risotto. As I stoop and pick, and pore over the big mushroom book, I feel Mark at my shoulder, pointing out the bulb at the bottom of the stem, or the way the gills are decurrent, extending down the stem, and maybe, behind him, the ghost of another man, one I never met, talking in accented English about the great forests of his youth.

Three years after Mark died, I was running up a little-used track that wound between sloping pastures and woods, filling in the half-hour before I had to collect Adam from his guitar lesson. It was a long, light evening in late summer, and a pair of buzzards called noisily from the woods that sprawled along the top of the hill. My eye was caught by an otherworldly array of pure white lumps curving across the field to my right. They looked like alien landing craft, and were mostly about the size of my head. So white, so beautiful, so unmistakable against the lush ripe green of the grazing land. Puffballs! Oh, Mark, look! Here they are, here they are – here they have been, all the time. I climbed the fence and picked one to take home for dinner, carrying it in my hands as I ran back to the car, because it was way too big for any pocket. It was lucky the lane was quiet, because I was crying so hard, I could hardly see.

ACKNOWLEDGEMENTS

Many thanks to my agent, Kirsty McLachlan, and my editor, Gill Fitzgerald-Kelly, for their faith in this book, their generosity and guidance throughout. I am also grateful to the other people at Picador who played a part in bringing this book to press, especially Laura Carr and Penelope Price. It has been much improved by their attention, and by that of my first readers and dear friends: Leslie Hill, Sarah Cameron, Richard Fay, Oliver Harris and Clare Anderson. Audrey Horning convinced me that my writing could become a book, and encouraged me to think that it was worth trying to find an agent and a publisher for it.

I am eternally grateful to my brother and sister, Ben Tarlow and Jo Maskill, and their families, and to all the friends mentioned here for letting me write about them. Thanks most of all to the best children in the East Midlands: Rachel, Adam and Greg. Mark would have been so proud to see what excellent adults you have turned into. Thanks also to all the other friends, colleagues and professionals who are not named here, but who supported us through the bad years and helped us find joy on the grimmest days.

The period since the time covered in this memoir has been

made sweet and wonderful in ways I would never have predicted, by the arrival in my life of Richard Dearden, whose love, intelligence, vitality and good company has never faltered, even though I was writing about my relationship with another man. Thank you.